Created by God—Purchased by Christ

Created by God— Purchased by Christ

Paula Rodriguez
with Lael Olsson

Tanglewood Publishing

Created by God—Purchased by Christ

By Paula Rodriguez

with Lael Olsson

Tanglewood Publishing
Clinton, Mississippi
1-800-241-4016

ISBN-13: 978-0-9793718-4-4

ISBN-10: 0-9793718-4-8

Cover Photo by Laura Rodriguez

Cover design by Sara Renick / Indigenous Designs

Book Layout and Design by Martha Nichols / aMuse Productions®

Printed in the United States of America

VERY SPECIAL THANKS

THE DOCTRINES OF GOD ARE SERIOUS THINGS, AND I WANTED TO MAKE sure that this study was as useful and theologically sound as possible, so I asked for two separate groups of opinions. The first group was asked to do the lessons and to critique the questions and answers. I would like to thank Barb Martin, Emily Prince, Andrea Perkins, and Emily Reeves for their help with this. One friend in particular went above and beyond, and she became my editor for this project. I first met Amy Carter when she was twelve or thirteen years old, and I was a friend of her mother. Amy has since earned a master's degree in English and is now a friend in her own right. She has been through every lesson, and she has not only answered all of the questions, but she has also edited all of the written work. Amy, I could not have done this without you.

For theological guidance, I turned to my many pastor and elder friends. Each one gave me valuable advice and encouragement. I would like to thank my husband, Charlie Rodriguez, and also John Allen, John Currid, Charles Dunahoo, Ken Elliott, Tim Fortner, Brian Kinney, Simon Kistemaker, Lou Lavallee, "Buck" Mosal, Gordon Reed, and John Reeves for helping me to make sure the comments in this study are theologically valid and in accordance with Scripture and the Westminster Standards.

TABLE OF CONTENTS

INTRODUCTION

THE *WESTMINSTER CONFESSION OF FAITH* AND THE SHORTER CATECHISM which grew out of it are statements of doctrine, of what many people believe are the teachings of the Bible. We who were involved in writing this study believe that they contain the best summary of what God has revealed to us through His Word. We also believe that if a person understands these teachings, they will bring much peace and comfort to his or her life in Christ. But we do not believe that understanding all of this doctrine is necessary to salvation.

The truths contained in the Shorter Catechism cannot be understood unless a person first has come to a saving knowledge of Jesus Christ. These truths are spiritually understood; they do not make sense to the human mind without the guidance of the Holy Spirit. If you have not yet established a personal relationship with Jesus Christ, this might not be the right time for this study. If you choose to continue with it, please remember that salvation comes first, then very slowly, the understanding of the knowledge of God.

The Shorter Catechism or the *Westminster Confession of Faith* is NOT the gospel. The Gospel is very simple: "Believe in the Lord Jesus Christ, and you will be saved." This means that we must understand that we are sinners and have broken the law of God, and that therefore we deserve to be punished. But Christ, in His mercy, took on our sins and died in our place. If we accept His death as punishment for our sins and agree to live in obedience to Him, out of our love and gratitude to Him, we will live forever with Him in eternity. That is the Gospel. The Shorter Catechism seeks to teach believers the doctrine of what we call the Reformed faith.

That is where this study comes in. Our goal is that by entering into this study, you will gain a better understanding of the teaching that is called the Reformed faith, which is contained in the *Westminster Confession of Faith* and the Larger and Shorter Catechisms.

There are some parts of the Shorter Catechism that are easy to understand and others that are very difficult. God leads each of us into understanding of this doctrine in our own time; so if there are things that seem too hard to take in, we encourage you to pray, search the Scripture, and then let God lead you in your own time as He directs. We also encourage you to be patient with others as they take their own individual journey through the mysteries of God's plan. Let God be God. He is much better at it than we are.

THE WESTMINSTER CONFESSION AND CATECHISMS

ON MAY 13, 1643, THE BRITISH PARLIAMENT ORGANIZED AN ASSEMBLY of ministers (or "divines") to create standards for a Church of England that would be reformed in worship, government, and doctrine. The Assembly comprised 151 members, including 30 laymen, chosen by Parliament to represent the counties, the universities, the House of Lords, and the House of Commons. Three were ministers of the Reformed Church of France, serving congregations in Canterbury and London. Twenty-eight did not attend, and twenty-one were appointed later to replace members who did not attend or who died during the proceedings.

The Westminster divines, mostly teachers and pastors of churches, were described by the Parliament as "learned, godly, and judicious." And they were. The Assembly's members were all Calvinists in theology; the main difference among them was in their views of church government and discipline. This resulted in a number of groups or parties—moderate Episcopalians (most of whom declined to attend out of loyalty to the king), Presbyterians (much the largest group), and Congregationalists.

The Assembly met at first in Westminster Abbey's imposing Henry VII Chapel. As the weather turned cooler, the divines were glad to move to the more comfortable Jerusalem Chamber. Every member took a vow to "maintain nothing in point of doctrine but what I believe to be most agreeable to the Word of God; nor in point of discipline, but what may make most for God's glory and the peace and good of his Church." The Assembly met every day except Saturday and Sunday, from nine o'clock until one or two. In the afternoons, the divines worked in committees. One of the rules guiding the deliberations required that "what any man undertakes to prove as necessary, he shall make good out of Scripture." The minutes and other reports of the Assembly's work reveal a strong commitment to this rule.

Much of the time of the Westminster divines was taken up with preaching and hearing sermons. Many hours were spent in corporate prayer and discussion concerning the lessons of God's providence. There were 1,163 numbered sessions of the Westminster Assembly, the last coming on February 22, 1649.

Over the course of five-and-a-half years, during a time of political and religious chaos, the Westminster Assembly created five great documents of theological orthodoxy and ecclesiastical stability for the church in England, Ireland, and Scotland.

The *Westminster Confession of Faith* is the Assembly's most important work. Drawing on the richness of the creeds and confessions of church history, the Westminster divines summed up in thirty-three chapters "what man is to believe concerning God, and what duty God requires of man." The Westminster Assembly also produced two catechisms—"one more exact and comprehensive, another more easy and short for new beginners." The Larger Catechism was completed in October 1647, and the Shorter Catechism a month later.

The Westminster Confession has been translated into many languages and has shaped Reformed churches and thought throughout the world. Its biblical faithfulness has helped many to know "how we may glorify and enjoy" God.

—excerpted from David B. Calhoun
"The Westminster Assembly."
The Confessions of Our Faith,
Fortress Edition, 2007

A NOTE TO WOMEN

WHY DOES A WOMAN NEED TO KNOW ABOUT THE SHORTER CATECHISM? Shouldn't we leave the doctrine up to the men of the church? Well, that depends on what you mean by doctrine and how you want it taught.

If by doctrine you mean the decisions about the official statements as to what a particular denomination believes, then, yes, many denominations believe that the Bible teaches that those decisions should be left up to the men. But there are denominations that include women in making those decisions. And although the *Westminster Confession of Faith* addresses this issue, the Shorter Catechism does not, so we will not address it in this discussion either. However, if by doctrine you mean the things we need to know and understand about God and Jesus Christ, then aren't these the things that we talk to our friends, family, and children about on a daily basis? I hope so. And how sad if our only answer to the questions of others is, "I don't know. You'll have to ask a man."

We certainly believe that women are intelligent enough to handle Biblical doctrine, and we think God believes so too. There are plenty of examples in the Bible to indicate this. Timothy was reminded by Paul to continue in the teaching he received from his mother and grandmother. Priscilla and Aquila are mentioned together; they worked hand-in-hand in spreading the Gospel. Many other women are commended by Paul in his letters to other Christians.

So let's not for a minute think that we don't have a place in doctrine. As I was writing this, I began to wonder why, if women are so instrumental in teaching doctrine to others, are most of the commands to teach our children given to men? Of course, God has given the ultimate responsibility for the household to the husband and father. But also, because it comes naturally to women to teach their children, there is no need for God to command us to do so. Proverbs 1:8 admonishes, "Hear, my son, your father's instruction, and forsake not your mother's teaching." It is just assumed that mothers will teach their children. But we do need to be certain that we are doing it right. That is the purpose of this study.

HOW TO USE THIS STUDY

AS A TEACHER, I ALWAYS WANT MY STUDENTS TO BE PREPARED WHEN they come to class. I want them to be familiar with the material before they hear what I have to say about it.

That is the way I have approached this study. First, I want you to be familiar with the material. I want you to see for yourself what Scripture has to say about these doctrines. I have done that by giving you questions to answer related to each of the Catechism questions. After you have answered the questions, then read what I have to say. Test what I say against what you have read. Your discussions will be much richer if you have prepared each lesson.

Finally, many people like to memorize the Catechism questions and answers. That is not my purpose, but I am not opposed to it. It is much more important, however, to understand the truths of the words than to memorize the words themselves.

The Shorter Catechism questions and answers used in this study are from the Fortress Edition, which is a standard English edition. This edition seeks to maintain the original wording of the Confession and Catechisms as often as possible, while updating archaic or obsolete language to make it more understandable to the modern reader.

If you have questions about the doctrines contained in these studies, please ask your pastor about them. I would also be happy to discuss these things with you via email. My address is *paula.catechism@gmail.com.*

1

LESSON 1
WHAT ARE WE HERE FOR?

Question 1: What is the chief end of man?
Answer: Man's chief end is to glorify God and to enjoy Him forever.

1. What does it mean that this is our *end*?
   Read Proverbs 16:4a; Isaiah 43:7

2. When should we glorify God?
   Read I Corinthians 10:31

3. What does it mean to glorify God?
   Read I Thessalonians 5:16-18; Acts 17:11; 2 John 6; I John 4:21

4. How long should we glorify God?
   Read Psalm 86:12

5. How can your life be more glorifying to God?

6. What does it mean to enjoy God?
   Read Psalm 73:25; Philippians 4:4-7

7. How long will we be able to enjoy Him?
   Read John 6:51; Revelation 22:3-5

8. What are some things in your life that are keeping you from truly enjoying God?

9. How can you change things in your life to be able to enjoy God more fully?

Question 2: What rule has God given to direct us how we may glorify and enjoy him?

Answer: The Word of God which is contained in the Scriptures of the Old and New Testaments is the only rule to direct us how we may glorify and enjoy him.

10. Where do the Scriptures come from?
Read 2 Timothy 3:16

11. What about other books that have been written after the Bible or in addition to the Bible?
Read Galatians 1:8; Revelation 22:18-19

12. How do we know the Old Testament is still valid?
Read Matthew 13:10-17. What is Jesus quoting in this passage?

Question 3: What do the Scriptures principally teach?

Answer: The Scriptures principally teach what man is to believe concerning God, and what duty God requires of man.

13. What can you learn from the Scriptures?
Read II Timothy 3:16

14. What truths have you learned from the Scriptures recently that can be helpful to you in glorifying or enjoying God?

LESSON 1
WHAT ARE WE HERE FOR?
Catechism Questions 1, 2, and 3

HAVE YOU EVER WONDERED WHY YOU WERE PUT ON THIS EARTH? Especially when you are afraid that your purpose might be to change dirty diapers or to drive carpool or to type memos for all eternity? Fortunately, God has a higher calling for all of us.

There is a popular poem by Langston Hughes called "The Creation" which portrays God as creating man because He is lonely; but let's be very clear about this—as much as I like Langston Hughes's poetry, and I do, God has never been lonely. There is nothing that God needs that He does not already possess. God does not need us in the same way that we need Him or that we need other people.

So why did He create us? The Bible tells us that He created us for His own purposes. He made us because He wanted to. Okay, but what does that tell us about our purpose? Simply that we have one. As the old saying goes, "God don't make no junk." Everything God makes has a purpose. So why were we created? God tells us through His Word that He created us for His glory, and therefore, that our purpose is first of all to glorify Him.

Great. If you are like me, you see the word glorify and it might as well be written in a foreign language. How in the world do you glorify someone? Do you walk around all day with your hands raised up saying, "I glorify you, O Lord!" You could, but I really don't think that's what God expects. I don't even think that would get the job done, because in saying the words, you would be missing opportunities to do the deed. Fortunately, the Bible does give us answers, so we are not left without any direction. (Actually, I have found that God very seldom leaves us without any direction, if we look for it. Often, we just don't want to look.)

There are many Scriptures that point to what it means to glorify God; but to condense it all down to one word, that word would be ***obedience***. When we obey God, we glorify Him, because we are giving Him first priority in our lives. This becomes especially important when our obedience to Him conflicts with what the rest of the world considers important. When we are faced with a choice between doing what our friends or co-workers think is the reasonable thing to do and doing what we know God would want us to do—what choice do we make? If we choose God's way, that is glorifying God.

If no one knows about our choice, if we are faced with a temptation to sin, but we call on God and ask Him to help us resist it—that is glorifying God.

If we make a habit of reading the Bible and praying—that is glorifying God.

If we teach our children, grandchildren, nieces, nephews, etc. about God—that is glorifying God.

If we thank God for everything that He gives us, even the little things that we might often take for granted—that is glorifying God.

And if we tell other people about the things that God has done for us—that is glorifying God.

What other examples can you think of?

As Pastor Rick Warren has said in his book *The Purpose Driven Life*, it's not about you. He is right, it's about God. But God cares about you, because another purpose God has for you is for you to enjoy Him. Have you ever thought about enjoying God? We talk about worshipping God, praying to God, serving God, extolling God, loving God, trusting God, believing God, thanking God, etc., but hardly ever do I hear anyone talk about *enjoying* God. Why not? I enjoy my husband, I enjoy my children, I enjoy my friends, I enjoy my co-workers (I have great co-workers!), I enjoy my fellow church members; why should I not enjoy God?

Marriage counselors tell us that we should enjoy our marriage partner because no one else knows us on such a deep and intimate level. But there are things that even my husband does not know. For instance, he does not know that when he puts the dishes away, I sometimes re-stack them because I do not like the way he does it. I will not ever criticize him for this because I am eternally grateful that he is so handy around the house, but I am also a really picky woman. (Okay, he knows now because he will read this. But there are lots of other things he does not know.) However, there is nothing that God does not know. If I were to tell you that I did not read my Bible this morning, but asked you not to tell God because I didn't want Him to find out, you would be justifiably concerned about my sanity. So if our relationship with God is the most intimate relationship we have, does it not follow that we should get the most enjoyment out of that relationship?

So how do we do that? First of all, to thoroughly enjoy God, He must be first in our hearts; He must take first place on our priority list. It is easy to put something or someone else in that place, but if we do that, then we can slip into the sin of worshipping that thing or that person instead of God. And we can see God as "interfering" with our plans for our lives with that thing or person.

I have three daughters, and I love them dearly. My idea of the perfect life could be that they all buy homes within a few minutes of mine and come over every evening with supper. (Notice that I did not say *for* supper. They all know that I am not fond of cooking.) However, God had other plans for them. None of them lives closer than a six hour drive from me. One lives in a different country. I could really resent that. I have to plan and pack and drive (or even fly) if I want to see them. But God has given our family so much fun and a wonderful son-in-law from a country I would never even have thought to visit. If God has first place, then we can enjoy Him and whatever plans He has for us.

Second, we need to not only accept what God has for us, but rejoice in it. As Paul tells us in his letter to the Philippians, we should present our requests to God because He wants us to communicate with Him, and part of that communication is telling Him what we want. But part of that communication should also be thanksgiving for what He has already done for us and given us. By reminding ourselves of what He has already given us, it will be easier to rejoice and enjoy Him in the future.

When I was in college, I thought I was in love. I prayed every night that God would allow me to marry the man of my dreams. One night I got an answer that was the nearest I have ever had to an audible answer from God. That answer was "No." I cried. I begged. I pleaded with God. The answer was still "No." I was convinced that my life was over. I knew this answer was from God. But I was in LOVE. I was miserable. I was certain that I would die lonely and unloved. I forgot to remember all of the blessings I had already received from God. Then I met the man who was to become my husband. As I got to know him better, I realized that although I had cared for the other young man, I had mistaken convenience and familiarity for love. My prayer then became that God would direct this new relationship. I prayed that if this was not the man God had for me, that I would be drawn away from him. Again God's answer was "No." I was not drawn away! We have now been married for thirty-two years. God's plans are always better than our own, because God is always smarter than we are!

We should rejoice always, but we need to be careful not to confuse joy with happiness. Happiness is a fleeting feeling of having what we want. Joy is a permanent feeling of knowing that everything is under control, even when we are not happy. It is possible to have joy even in the midst of deep sorrow, when we know that even though we don't understand the reason for our distress, there is a God who has everything under control. It is this underlying joy that makes our suffering bearable. I write this with great trepidation, because I have not even begun to master this. I will not set myself up as an example. I am not. I only know of others who have been examples to me. I know of a friend who faced her imminent death from ovarian cancer with a grace and serenity that could only have come from a deep and abiding joy in the Lord. I have acquaintances who were never supposed to have been able to have a second child. When they miraculously conceived their precious daughter, they lost her soon after her birth to a rare genetic disorder. It can only be because of a deep faith and joy in the love of their God that they were able to survive that loss and to continue on to raise their son and later an adopted child to know and love the Lord as they do. And I know that in the deaths of people who were very precious to me, of whose salvation I was not at all certain, I was kept from utter despair only because of the certainty that there is a God who knows the end from the beginning and who has everything under control and keeps me close in His sovereign hand.

Not only do we glorify God and get to enjoy Him, but it lasts forever! We will live forever! Think of it. Of course, if forever weren't any better than the life I have now, there are times I wouldn't want it. But our forever will be perfect. Forever begins now and continues into the next life, without sin, sickness, or sorrow. That's the kind of forever I can look forward to. And that's the kind of forever God promises us we will have. Our job is simply to glorify and enjoy Him.

How do we know that this is all true? The answer comes from one of the most basic of all Christian hymns, one that every one of us probably learned when we were children, "The Bible tells me so." The Bible is the literal Word of God, meaning that God the Holy Spirit guided and directed what the men who wrote it were to write. One of the most amazing things about the Bible is that even though it was written over many centuries by many different people, it is consistent in its teaching and its story. Through the Scriptures in the Bible, we can learn about God and how we can best serve and glorify Him [teaching]. We can also learn what we are doing that does not glorify Him [reproof] and how we can change that [correction]. And we can learn how to be the person that God has intended us to be [training in righteousness].

There are other books that claim to be messages from God, or divinely inspired books, but isn't it astounding! Even before any of those other books were written, God knew about them and warned us against them. Everything we need to know about God and everything that is true about God has been given to us in His Word. We can turn to others to help us understand His Word, but we must be very cautious whenever anyone adds to or takes away from what is written there.

Finally, let me say a word about the Old Testament. How do we know that it is still valid? There are some churches which call themselves "New Testament" churches and do not consider the Old Testament to be relevant to our lives today. However, there are many, many examples of instances where an Old Testament passage is quoted in the New Testament. In many cases, these passages are quoted by Christ Himself. I think it is safe to assume that if Christ considered the Old Testament to be valid, we can as well. The entire Bible, from beginning to end, is a picture of God's relationship with His people. We cannot ignore anything that God wants to tell us, no matter where in His Word it is located.

2

LESSON 2
WHAT IS GOD LIKE?

Question 4: What is God?

Answer: God is a Spirit, infinite, eternal, and unchangeable, in his being, wisdom, power, holiness, justice, goodness, and truth.

1. What does it mean that God is infinite?
   Read Job 11:7-9; I Kings 8:27;

2. What does it mean that God is eternal?
   Read Psalm 90:2,10:16

3. What does it mean that God is unchangeable?
   Read James 1:17; Hebrews 13:8

4. How is God infinite, eternal, and unchangeable in His being?
   Read Psalm 139:7-10; Revelation 22:13; Hebrews 13:8

5. How is God infinite, eternal, and unchangeable in His wisdom and power?
   Read Jeremiah 51:15; Psalm 147:5; Daniel 7:14

6. How is God infinite, eternal, and unchangeable in his holiness?
   Read Psalm 111:9; Isaiah 6:3; Revelation 4:8; Numbers 23:19

7. How is God infinite, eternal, and unchangeable in his justice?
   Read Psalm 33:5-6, Zephaniah 3:5

8. How is God infinite, eternal, and unchangeable in his goodness?
   Read Psalm 100:5; Malachi 3:6

9. How is God infinite, eternal, and unchangeable in his truth?
   Read John 14:16-17; I Peter 1:23-25

Question 5: Are there more Gods than one?

Answer: There is but one only, the living and true God.

10. What does it mean that God is a living God?
    Read Jeremiah 10:9-11; 2 Corinthians 6:16

11. What does it mean that God is the true God?
    Read Deuteronomy 4:39

Question 6: How many Persons are there in the Godhead?

Answer: There are three Persons in the Godhead: the Father, the Son, and the Holy Spirit; and these three are one God, the same in substance, equal in power and glory.

12. Where in Scripture do we see the three persons of the Godhead referred to together?
    Read Matthew 3:16-17; 28:19; 2 Corinthians 13:14

LESSON 2
WHAT IS GOD LIKE?
Catechism Questions 4, 5, and 6

IT IS HARD TO FATHOM WHAT OR WHO GOD IS. MY DAUGHTER LAEL has heard many different descriptions of God while working with a campus ministry in Europe. The students at the university where she worked prided themselves on their knowledge, openness to all ideas, and ability to think "critically;" so when asked the question "Who is God?" the campus workers got a wide range of, umm, "critically-thought-through" answers. One answer was that God is a woman in the sky who does not judge anyone. Another said God is someone who helps us when we need it. Some believed that we create God ourselves according to our own personal beliefs. All of the answers were only half-hearted attempts to describe something that the students had never really considered because they were afraid of facing the truth and exploring something unknown. People are afraid to face the idea of God, because if there is a God, then they are subject to Him.

What is God like? To begin with, God is a Spirit; He does not have a body—not a man's body or a woman's body. He is not an old man or an old woman sitting in the sky looking down on us.

No one has ever seen the Spirit (unless there are some who may have seen Him in visions), but all of us have seen the effects of the Spirit. Jesus compared the work of the Spirit to the effects of the wind,[1] and Billy Graham likes to expand on this idea. We cannot see the wind when it blows, but we can see what the wind does. We see the leaves blowing and we know that the wind is there because of the effects we see. God is everywhere, and we can know He is there by the things He does in the world and in our lives. God's Spirit is too wonderful and terrifying for us to see; it would be too overwhelming for our human eyes to bear. However, we can see the wonders that He performs. God's Spirit is with us everywhere; He has no limits.

Although there is only one God, that God exists in three distinct persons. This is an aspect of the nature of God that all other religions have failed to recognize. Many people like to believe that everyone basically worships the same god regardless of the precise religion they follow, but that is simply not true. (Of course I am talking about major world religions here, not various Christian denominations.) All other religions either acknowledge more than one god or fail to acknowledge all three persons of the Godhead, which we call the Trinity. To do either of these things is to fail to worship the true God.

How do we know that God exists in three persons? Because Christ Himself told us so. In Matthew 28:19, He specifically instructed us to baptize believers in the name of the Father and of the Son and of the Holy Spirit. He told us that He and the Father are one[2] and that He would send us the Holy Spirit, who proceeds from the Father.[3] John also tells us in his first letter "For there are three that bear witness in heaven: the Father, the Word, and the Holy Spirit; and these three are one." (I John 5: 7) Because of what he wrote in his Gospel, we know that by "the Word" John is referring to Christ.

So how does that work, exactly? How can there be one God in three persons? I have absolutely no idea. Rumor has it that in our presbytery, when men were being examined for ordination, a particular seminary professor used to like to ask the question, "Can you explain the Trinity?" This was actually a trick question because the correct answer is "No." We cannot explain the Trinity. Every time we try, we not only fall far short of a good explanation, we usually end up committing one or more serious doctrinal errors. The problem is that our minds are too small to understand the ways of God. But rather than being upset by this, we should be comforted. I will probably say this many times during this study, but I am extremely glad that I cannot understand everything about God. I want God to know much more than I know and to understand things that I cannot possibly understand. If God's abilities were limited only to the things I can understand, He would be a very weak and limited God, and that is not the kind of God I need or want. And fortunately, that is not the kind of God He is. God is not limited by what I know, by what I understand, or even by the things that limit me.

For example, God is not limited by time as I am because He has always existed in the past and will exist forever in the future. He is never in a hurry to get things done because He is afraid He will run out of time. Why? Because He created time! Look at Jesus' own words, "Before Abraham was, I am!" (John 8:58) Jesus did not say "I was" for a reason; God exists in the past, present, and future all at the same time. This is hard for us to understand because we exist within the time that God created. We have no understanding of something without a beginning or an end. When Lael was little, she would lie in her bed at night and think about how God did not have an end, and how, when we are with Him, we also do not have an end. This was so big for her little mind to understand that she would literally start crying and run to Mom and Dad for comfort. Our human minds simply cannot wrap around ideas of infinity and eternity because we had a definite beginning and we see so many endings.

God had no beginning and He has no end, and throughout all time God has never changed. His nature is exactly the same today as it was thousands of years ago. The God who spoke to Moses is the same God who is with us today. His attributes have not changed. God never gets any wiser or more powerful because He has always been as wise and as powerful as anything could ever be. His holiness has not decreased; He is still holy, holy, holy. God is still a just God, and in His wisdom He reigns with justice. We live in a world where people like to take situations into their own hands and do what they think is best, but God is the only pure and wise judge. We know that His justice will continue through all eternity and that He is the one who will right all wrongs.

God's goodness is so beautiful. His goodness has never changed; He wants the best for his children. He will never stop being a good God. Isn't that wonderful? Sometimes I have trouble remembering God's complete goodness. I see all the destruction in the world and it is easy to forget that we have a loving and good God who is there in the midst of it all. But because God's truth never changes and never diminishes, we know that we can trust that no aspect of God will ever change and that all of His words are forever true. He will always be there to love us unconditionally, to be with us in times of trouble, and to keep us on the right path.

Lael and I wish that the students she talked to could understand who God truly is. Instead they are limited by the fear of giving up control of their lives. We understand how frightening it is to give up control, but if we recognize who God truly is, then it is not frightening at all—because God is the one person we can totally and completely trust in and count on.

3

LESSON 3
HOW BIG IS YOUR GOD?

Question 7: What are the decrees of God?

Answer:* *The decrees of God are His eternal purpose, according to the counsel of His will, by which, for His own glory, He has foreordained whatever comes to pass.

1. How much control does God have?
   Read Daniel 4:35

2. Is God impulsive in what He does?
   Read Isaiah 46:10; 55:11; Proverbs 19:21

3. Does God have purposes for people?
   Read Exodus 9:16; Jeremiah 29:11

4. What does it mean that God has foreordained things?
   Read Isaiah 55:11; Jeremiah 1:5

5. What things has God foreordained?
   Read Proverbs 16:4

6. What difference does it make to know that God has a purpose for your life?

Question 8: How does God execute His decrees?

Answer: God executes His decrees in the works of creation and providence.

7. What things did God create?
   Read Psalm 104:5-24

8. How did He create everything?
   Read Psalm 33:6-9

9. How does creation glorify God?
   Read Psalm 19:1; Psalm 104:12-13, 27-28, 31

10. How does God exercise His providence over us?
    Read Psalm 73: 24

11. How does this glorify God?
    Read John 16:13-14

12. In what ways have you been aware of the guidance of the Holy Spirit in your own life?

LESSON 3
HOW BIG IS YOUR GOD?
Catechism Questions 7 and 8

WHEN OUR CHILDREN WERE LITTLE, MY HUSBAND AND I USED TO TEACH classes in the Children's Catechism. The first question is "Who made you?" and the answer is "God." Really easy. And everybody got it right on the first day, even the very young ones. But the second question—oh my!

It sounds simple enough—"What else did God make?" The answer is "God made all things." Still pretty simple, right? For grown ups. But children are so literal. Almost every child we ever taught answered that question with a list—"God made flowers and trees and bunnies and penguins and oatmeal and mommies and butterflies and sandwiches and cars and milk...." You get the idea. But how do you correct them? They aren't wrong. God did make those things. We want them to understand that God made all things (we just don't want them to try to list them!).

Why did God do this? Simply because He wanted to. He had, and still has, a purpose for creating everything that He has created. (There are a few things that I am still wondering about, like those creatures that I sometimes have to exterminate out of my house, but I will have to trust that there is some kind of eternal purpose for them too.) The important thing here is purpose. Nothing, I repeat, NOTHING, on this earth exists here by chance, by accident. Everything is here to fulfill a purpose of God.

That can be hard to imagine in light of some of the horrible things that happen in today's world. But those same horrible things have happened ever since the beginning of time. Think of the first crime ever committed—a man killed his own brother because of jealousy. Not long after that and we have rape, incest, child sacrifice, and everything else that you can imagine. As Solomon says in Ecclesiastes, "There is nothing new under the sun."

God knows about these things, and He can use these things for His purposes too. We may not be able to see how, but that is one reason that I am glad He is God and I am not. I am not smart enough to take these horrible events and make any good at all come out of them, but God can. God can see the end from the beginning, and He can orchestrate events so that good can triumph over evil, even if we never see it happen.

Have you ever stopped to think about what this means in your own life? You were created for a purpose. Before you were born, or even formed in your mother's womb, God had a purpose for you. God knew who you would be, what your name would be, where you would grow up, and under what circumstances. Some of us would have preferred to grow up in circumstances other than the ones we had. But we have to remember that God had a purpose in everything that happened to us. And His purpose is for our ultimate good. In Jeremiah 29:11 God tells us that His plans are to give us a hope and a future. Those are good plans. If you have been through hard times, I do not in any way want to minimize the pain and suffering you have been through. I would not pretend to try to explain what God's purpose was in allowing those things to happen. I am not nearly as wise as God. I will only tell you that I am absolutely positive that God's ultimate plan for you is good.

I also know that God created you for that good plan. Romans 9:23-24 tells us that we who believe in Christ are not just allowed to share in Christ's glory, but we were actually created for that very purpose! Does that make you proud? It shouldn't. We had absolutely nothing to do with it. Just like you had nothing to do with your skin color or hair color (your *original* hair color!) or eye color, you had nothing to do with being created to share in Christ's glory. God did it all. It's nothing to brag about. It is something to thank God for.

Let's think about creation for a minute. There are those who want to leave God out of the picture, who want to leave it all up to chance. I don't want to dwell on the details of creation too much because we will take that up in the next lesson, but honestly, it takes much more faith to believe this all just "bloomed" into being. As a former pastor used to explain, if you were driving along the road and saw a random pile of boards, nails, and shingles, would you assume that was a house coming into being or a house falling down? Most of us would assume the house was falling down. Houses come into being in a more orderly manner. Usually the lumber is neatly stacked, the nails are in boxes, and the shingles are in boxes or stacks as well. Admittedly, there are messy contractors, but you get my point. Things come into being in an orderly way.

First, you build the foundation, then the support beams, etc. You don't just mix up the boards and wait for a house to grow.

Most people who want to take God out of the picture of the formation of the world do so because they want to take God out of the picture of their lives. If God was there at creation, then He is probably still there. And if He is still there, He might expect something from them, and that might make them uncomfortable. So if they can explain God away from the beginning of things, then maybe they can make him cease to exist altogether.

If only logic really worked that way! If only I could make things cease to exist just because I don't want them to! Then my friend who died of cancer would not have died because I could have refused to believe the cancer existed, and it would have been gone. And my nephew whose wife left him could have refused to believe there was a problem in his marriage, and everything would have been fine. We could all live according to the motto on a dish towel my sister gave me: "Better living through denial."

Please don't read this and think I don't want God to exist. I am simply pointing out the absurdity of thinking that if I don't believe in Him, I can make Him go away. But as the title of one of Dr. Francis Schaeffer's books reads, "God is there and He is not silent." Refusing to believe in Him will not make Him go away. And there is not one shred of scientific evidence that disproves the existence of God and the "miraculous" appearance of life without intelligent interference, i.e. evolution. I do not have space to go into this argument here, but I will give a list of books at the end of this study that you can consult if you would like to do further reading.

God exists. He created everything simply by speaking it into being. And all of creation exists to glorify God, which it does, although imperfectly, because we live in an imperfect, fallen world. Which leads to the question—as part of His creation, are you doing your part to glorify Him?

But amazingly, that is not the only purpose God had in creating us. He also created each one of us to allow us to share in His glory. Wow! I can't believe I just wrote that. But it is absolutely true.

That would be enough, but God's providence means that He doesn't leave us alone to figure things out on our own. He guides us through this mess we call life. Have you ever thought about how messy life really is? People do not behave the way they are supposed to. I was talking with some friends the other night, and we were discussing how much better life would be if everyone would just obey the Golden Rule (Do to others as you would have them do to you). But we can't even get that right. So life gets messy. We have to deal with those people. And sometimes we are those people.

But God is still there with us in all the mess.

Have you ever smelled a skunk? Many of you know what skunks look, and more importantly, smell like. If you don't, imagine the worst thing you have ever smelled in your life. Now mix that with vinegar. That's skunk. When my youngest daughter was in college, she told me about a time when a skunk wandered onto the campus. One young man decided to try to catch it. He was not successful, but he got close. You can imagine the results. His roommate, in fact his whole dorm, was not amused. He smelled for days. He was pretty unpopular for a while.

Now imagine that was your four-year-old son. What would you do? You would have to help him. You couldn't stay away, because he wouldn't be able to take care of himself. So you would have to face the smell and deal with it. That's what God does. He can't stay away, because we can't take care of ourselves. We are like little children, and He cares too much for us to let us flounder about on our own. So He deals with the smells and the muck and whatever else we get ourselves into and cleans us up and puts us back on the right track until we mess up again.

Now if that guy had asked for advice, such as, "Do you think I should try to catch that skunk?" I'm sure someone would have given him some much-needed wisdom. Some of those students had undoubtedly smelled skunk before and didn't want to smell it again. And if we ask God for wisdom, He also promises to give it. We just have to remember to take time to ask. But too often we are so attracted by the pretty white stripe that we forget to ask if it's really good for us. And we end up suffering the consequences. But we never suffer alone. God is always with us.

So if we want to ask for advice, where do we find the counsel of God? We must always find His counsel in a way that is glorifying to Him. So first, we should look to His own Word in the Scriptures. We should be reading the Bible every day. We can often find the exact answer to the very question we have in our reading for that day. Or a good concordance can help us to find Bible verses which contain specific words. Other Bible study aids can help us to find passages on particular subjects.

Second, we can pray and ask God to direct us, but we need to be careful with this. We must be sure that the answer we think is from God is not in conflict with what is revealed in His Word. We must also be sure that we are ready to hear what God has to say. I had two dear aunts who are now with Jesus. They both loved the Lord, and on one visit to my family in Louisiana, they had a conflict. Aunt Sarah had driven there from Oklahoma and Aunt Jane had taken the bus from Arkansas. Aunt Jane wanted Aunt Sarah to take her home, but Aunt Sarah didn't want to. They decided to go into separate rooms to pray about it and see how God led them. After prayer, they came out and Aunt Jane said that God had revealed to her that Aunt Sarah should indeed drive her home. Aunt Sarah said that God had told her that Aunt Jane should take the bus. If you are going to pray, you have to be prepared to listen to God, not your own selfish desires. Sometimes our selfishness can yell so loud we don't allow ourselves to hear the clear, authoritative voice of God.

In addition to prayer, you can ask Christian friends. But again, we must be careful that they have our best interests and the truth of God at heart and not their own agenda. Cultivate godly friends who search the Scriptures for answers for their own lives, and they will do the same for you. And be certain you are asking Christian friends. People who are living to glorify God do not see the world in the same way that others do. We need advice from people who understand our purpose in the world and who know and love the God who created and sustains us.

God has a purpose for this world, and that purpose has not changed since the beginning of time. Part of that purpose was to create you to share in His glory. And having created you, He is still with you every step of the way. Listen to His voice and follow his guidance. He will lead you to your hope and your future, for His glory.

4

LESSON 4
WHO MADE YOU?

Question 9: What is the work of creation?

Answer: The work of creation is God's making all things from nothing, by the word of His power, in the space of six days, and all very good.

1. What does it mean that God made all things from nothing?
   Read Genesis 1:2; Hebrews 11:3

2. How did God create all things except man?
   Read Genesis 1: 3, 6, 9, 11, 14, 20, 24

3. How is a day defined in the Creation passage?
   Read Genesis 1: 5, 8, 13, 19, 23, 31

4. In what order did God create the world?
   Read Genesis 1: 3, 6, 9, 11, 14, 20, 24, 26

5. Why was everything good?
   Read Genesis 1:4, 10, 12, 18, 21, 25, 31; Psalm 19:1; Psalm 104:16-28

6. How was the Holy Spirit involved in creation?
   Read Genesis 1:2

7. How was Christ involved in creation?
   Read John 1:1-3, 14

8. How is the Triune God made evident in the Creation story?
   Read Genesis 1:26

9. How did God create man?
   Read Genesis 2:7

10. How did God create woman?
    Read Genesis 2:21-22

11. If you are a creation of God, and not a product of evolutionary chance, what difference does that make in your life?

LESSON 4
WHO MADE YOU?
Catechism Question 9

THERE ARE FEW ISSUES IN THE CHRISTIAN FAITH THAT CAN STIR UP AS much controversy between believers and non-believers, and even among Christians, as the issue of Creation. Did God really create the earth? What about evolution? Hasn't science proved that all of life evolved from primitive organisms? And couldn't God have used evolution to create what now exists on earth?

I cannot possibly answer these questions in detail. Whole books have been written by men and women who are far more knowledgeable than I about such matters, and you can find a list of such books at the end of this study guide. However, I will touch on some of the basics.

First of all, since Scripture is to be our guide for all of life, then we must look to Scripture first; and Scripture tells us that God did indeed create everything in six days. There was absolutely nothing in existence other than God before Creation; there was an entire universe in existence afterward. We are given a fairly brief but detailed account of how it was done. God spoke, and things sprang into being. That is a miracle. But since God is in the business of miracles, we shouldn't be surprised.

Let's consider the alternative for a moment. First of all, let's define the term *evolution*. There are two major types of "evolution" to consider. Number one is something that most scientists, even creationists, agree on. Plants and animals do change over time. For example, in England there was a species of moth that came in black and white varieties. Since the white variety blended in better with the tree bark, the birds could see more of the black ones. More of the black ones got eaten, so there were more white ones. When the industrial revolution came along, the factories put out so much smoke that the trees were covered with black soot. All of a sudden the black moths were hidden and the white moths were easier for the birds to see. Now there were more black moths. That is a version of evolution called natural selection. Aspects of a creature that make it better able to adapt to its environment get carried on in its gene pool, and more and more of the creature have that characteristic. But the key is that the basic creature does not change into another creature. A moth is still a moth, a snail is still a snail, etc.

The second type of evolution is the problem. According to this theory, at one time there was a mass of something (matter, energy?) which suddenly exploded. This begs the question of where the mass of something came from, but let's proceed anyway. Eventually some of this stuff cooled off and formed spheres and some of it remained hot and formed stars. Or maybe the hot stuff spun off matter that then cooled off. Anyway, because of gravitational pull, the cool stuff began to rotate around the hot stuff, and we had solar systems. And also because of gravity, these solar systems were attracted to one another, and grouped together to form galaxies.

On some of these cool places (or maybe just one of them), where conditions were just exactly right, the exact right combination of hydrogen and oxygen formed in sufficient quantities to produce water. A little while later, the exact right combination of other elements combined to produce small cell-like structures, which then mutated to become living cells, which then combined and mutated until they became primitive organisms. These primitive organisms then mutated over and over again until they became more advanced organisms, and finally, primitive man developed. Man became more and more advanced until we are what we are today.

This is where creation science and evolutionary science part company. And yes, there are many reputable scientists who believe in Creation. In fact there are many scientists who find that true science provides much more evidence for the concept of Creation than for the idea of evolution.

Consider the odds of something like this actually happening. Let's look at the possibility of the formation of just one tiny part of a living cell—amino acids. The chance of the random generation of even one amino acid capable of existing in a living cell is 10 to the 123rd power. In other words, 1 chance in 10 followed by 123 zeros (i.e. 1 in 1,000,000,000,000,000,000,000,000,000,000,000,000,000, 000,000,000,000,000,000,000,000,000,000,000,000,000,000,000,000,000, 000,000,000,000,000,000,000,000,000,000,000,000,000). The odds of winning the lottery are 1 in 80,000,000. And to sustain a living cell, this would need to happen 500 times.[4] What a miracle! But wait—this is science. Evolutionary science has no room for miracles. And these are the odds for just one of the millions of building blocks of life.

This sounds highly unlikely to me. But let's assume, for the sake of argument, that we hit the cosmic jackpot and actually got enough amino acids to create a living cell. There are still a lot of major roadblocks standing in the way of creating a human being, or anything remotely close.

First, there is the problem of going from the single cell to the multi-cellular, extremely complex organism called man. This would require that single cell to differentiate itself over and over again to form different organs and systems of the body. Many evolutionists want to explain this differentiation using the concept of mutation. The problem is that according to science, beneficial mutations do not occur. Mutations produce genetic abnormalities which are harmful, or even fatal, to an organism. But for random processes to have caused man to come into existence, such beneficial mutations would have had to occur thousands, if not millions, of times.

Second, there is a pesky little thing called the Second Law of Thermodynamics. It sounds complicated, but it's really not. To begin with, a Law is something that we really do know is true—like the Law of Gravity. We know that if we throw something into the air, it will fall down. Always. Every time. That's why it's called a Law.

The Second Law of Thermodynamics basically tells us that in a closed system (one that is not acted on by an outside force), there will be more and more disorder and less and less ability to do work until there is no more ability to do any work at all. In other words, things wind down until they stop. For the universe and all it contains to have come into being through random processes, the universe must have had less disorder and more order, or in other words, the universe would have had to wind up and go faster and faster. That just doesn't happen. Not ever.

If the universe were created by God, however, the Second Law of Thermodynamics would not even apply. The universe would no longer be a closed system, since it would be acted upon by an outside force [God] and given the extra energy needed to do the job of creating and sustaining life.

So let's accept the fact that God did create the universe and everything in it, including us. How did He do it? He simply spoke, and it came into being. I was going to say we can only imagine—but I don't think we really can. In his book *The Magician's Nephew*, C. S. Lewis gives us a beautiful allegorical picture of what that might have looked like. Read Job 38:4-11 for God's own description of His work of creation. And He proclaimed that it was good.

How do you define good? Too often I consider something good if it's good for me—if I like it or want it or it makes me happy. But I don't think that's God's definition. I don't think that when the Bible says that God saw that something was good, it means that it made God happy. I do think it means that it pleased Him.

So what pleases God? According to I Samuel 12:23-24, it would be fearing the Lord and serving Him faithfully; in other words, obedience. When God created each thing, He gave it a purpose and told each thing what to do. And everything did as it was told; everything in all creation was perfectly obedient to God's command. So everything was perfectly good.

I have not yet touched on another tricky part of this whole story—the six days bit. Did God really create the entire universe in six days? Let me ask you a question—Could God have created the universe in six days?

If your answer is no, or even, I'm not sure, then you are not giving God enough credit. Of course He could. He is God. He is all-powerful. He can do anything He desires to do. Nothing is impossible for God. Whether He could do it should not be up for discussion. But there is some question among godly and intelligent Bible scholars about whether He did.

I am not going to try to pretend that I know more than my brothers and sisters in Christ who have studied this far more than I have. I would just ask us all to be careful as we consider this issue and be sure we are letting our study of the Bible guide our study of "science" and not the other way around. In my own humble opinion, if God could do it, and the Bible says He did do it, there is no reason to believe He did not do it.

Throughout this discussion I have been talking about God creating the universe. What does the term God bring to your mind? God the Father? Sometimes we forget that the entire Trinity has always existed and will always exist. God—Father, Son, and Holy Spirit—created us. John makes it crystal clear that we are created by Christ, that He existed in the beginning and was and is God the Creator. Genesis refers to the Spirit of God being involved in the act of Creation.

I am a teacher of communication, and one of the basics of communication is that human beings have an innate need to communicate. John McCain is quoted as saying that when he was a prisoner of war, the men would risk torture and even death to communicate with one another. Most women have an innate need to communicate; we find particular pleasure in the act of communicating. Anyway, as a communication teacher, I find Genesis 1:26 fascinating. God said, "Let us make man in our image." Who was He talking to? To Himself. God has perfect fellowship with Himself. He doesn't need anyone else to communicate with because He has Himself.

I am not saying that I understand this. I absolutely do not. How the Trinity exists and operates is totally beyond the ability of my tiny brain to comprehend. But that actually gives me a great deal of comfort. The fact that I cannot understand God means that God is infinitely more wise and knowledgeable than I am, and that is the kind of God I want and need.

And this God, who did not and still does not need anyone or anything, chose to create you in His image. Of all of the millions of creatures He created, you are the one He created in a unique and special way. You are the one he formed from the dust of the ground, or from the rib of man, and into whom He breathed the breath of life. You are the one He created in His likeness. You are the one with whom He has a special bond.

What is your response to His creation? Do you understand how special this makes you? Does this humble you to know that the God who created the entire universe in six days, merely by speaking, loves you and desires fellowship with you? Can you respond to this awesome knowledge with the obedience that God desires and that He will call good?

5

LESSON 5
WHAT'S A PERSON TO DO?

Question 10: How did God create man?

Answer: ***God created man male and female, after His own image, in knowledge, righteousness, and holiness, with dominion over the creatures.***

1. Is either man or woman more important to God?
   Read Genesis 1:27-28; Galatians 3:28

2. Describe the godly widow in I Timothy 5:9-10.

3. Describe the godly woman in Proverbs 31:13-25.

4. How do each of these women reflect the image of God?
   Read Nahum 1:7; Isaiah 61:10; Psalm 104:14

5. How are we to exercise dominion over the creatures?
   Read I Timothy 5:18; Genesis 9:3; Proverbs 12:10

6. How does your life reflect the image of God?

Question 11: What are God's works of providence?

Answer: God's works of providence are His most holy, wise, and powerful preserving and governing all His creatures, and all their actions.

7. How does God preserve His creation?
   Read Hebrews 1:3; Job 39-41; Matthew 6:26-28

8. How does God govern His creation?
   Read Job 38:8-11, 35; 39:5-8, 26-29; Mark 4:35-41

9. How does God preserve His people?
   Read Psalm 121:8; Psalm 1:1-3

10. Does God preserve only His chosen people, or all people?
    Read Matthew 5:45, 6:31-33

11. How does God govern His people?
    Read Exodus 20:1-17; Job 12:23; Proverbs 3:6; Psalm 92:9

12. What is your response to the knowledge that God governs His creation?

LESSON 5
WHAT'S A PERSON TO DO?
Catechism Questions 10 and 11

I HAD A STUDENT A FEW YEARS AGO WHO WAS IN HER MID-THIRTIES. She explained to me that she was going to college at this time in her life because her father had not let her go when she was younger. His opinion was that a girl only needed a high school education. After that, her role was to get married, have babies, and let her husband take care of her. I was stunned. I associated that kind of thinking with Jane Austen novels. I had no idea it still existed.

How does God view the role of women? Let's look at a few Scriptures. In Genesis, we have the examples of Sarah, Rebekah, Leah, and Rachel, who worked at home caring for their families. In the New Testament, we see the same types of examples in the lives of Mary the mother of Jesus, Elizabeth, and Martha. On the other hand, Proverbs 31 paints a picture of a wife and mother who takes care of her household and at the same time works as a very successful merchant. One of the judges of Israel was Deborah.[5] In Acts 16, we are told that the first Christian convert in Macedonia was Lydia, a seller of purple goods. We are never told that she was admonished to stop selling her wares. In Acts 18, we are introduced to Aquila and Priscilla, and we are told that they were tentmakers by trade. Later in that same chapter, we read that both Priscilla and Aquila instructed Apollo in the ways of God more accurately. Interestingly, Priscilla is mentioned first here.

Why then does Peter refer to women as the "weaker vessel"?[6] I think because it's the truth. Generally speaking, women are not as physically strong as men. That's why there are separate events for women and men in sporting events such as the Olympics. Women are also more emotional, as a rule. For example, we cry more easily. Women are generally more tender-hearted, which can make them more vulnerable to the deception of others. Peter is telling men to be understanding of this because that is the way God created us. Notice that Peter does not say "less intelligent vessel" or "less deserving vessel" or "less capable vessel." Please do not extrapolate meanings from the term "weaker" that God did not intend it to have. If He had meant less intelligent, etc., He would have said so.

So what about the idea that a woman's place is in the home? Where did that come from? Well, first of all, for most of history, everyone's place was in the home. All of the work, whatever it was, was done in the home. Somewhere along the way, men realized that they could leave the home, not being tied down with nursing babies, so they established places of business elsewhere. So it is basically a tradition that has come down to us from fairly recent history. I can find nothing in Scripture that commands that it is the mother who must do the majority of the child-rearing in the family. In fact, almost all of the Scriptures dealing with the raising of children are directed to the fathers.

In the country of Sweden, where Lael lives, they are trying to create a balance in child-rearing. When a couple has a child, both parents get seven months of child-care leave at 80% of their salary, with guaranteed re-employment at the end of the leave. Fathers must take at least two months of that leave and are encouraged to take their full seven months. This means that in Sweden, no child is away from a parent for at least the first year of life. Now there are many things about Swedish parenting laws that I have questions about, but this is something I can really support, especially when I see six-week-old babies in day-care because their mothers have no choice but to return to work if they are going to be able to financially make ends meet.

I suppose the point I am trying to make, in a very roundabout way, is that God created both male and female, and neither is less valuable to Him, nor less capable of serving Him. Nor has He limited what either gender can do in their service of Him, other than in certain roles in the church. Every once in a while I hear well-meaning Christians admonishing others, especially women, about life choices they have made. I think we need to be very careful about this. There are no instructions in Scripture about exactly what roles a woman is to take in society at large. There are examples of women who worked outside the home and women who worked in the home. Both can be valid and godly choices. Some women remain single and have fulfilling careers. Some women choose to stay at home and devote themselves full-time to the care of their families. Some choose to divide their time between family and career. Some even work full-time outside the home while their husbands stay home full-time and care for their children. It is up to each family to prayerfully consider what God would have them do, and it is up to other individuals and families to stay out of each others' business, unless they are specifically asked for advice. God does not give us the knowledge to judge each other's activities; in fact, He admonishes us against it.[7]

God may not have given us the knowledge to meddle in each other's lives, but He does give us knowledge of Himself and His Word. And if both male and female are created in God's image in knowledge, with no distinction, does it not follow that both are capable of understanding the things of God? Not as many women as men have formal seminary training, but women can read. And women need to study doctrine, formally or not. Not to do so is to be without necessary knowledge. That is part of the purpose of this study—to encourage both men and women in the understanding of the truths of our faith. There are lots of other good books out there, and we are all capable of understanding them.

Now if anyone has not become a new creature in Christ, then that's a different story. Godly knowledge is for God's people. If a person does not have the Spirit of God as his guide, he cannot understand the knowledge of God. It is incomprehensible and sometimes offensive to him. So in our evangelistic efforts, let's keep this in mind. Unsaved people need Jesus; they do not need the five points of Calvinism. My husband and I once met with a group of young Christians who were trying to start a Presbyterian church in their small town. They were very sincere in their beliefs, but perhaps a little over-zealous. One young woman confided in me that she had been witnessing to someone at work and was trying to explain to her the doctrine of limited atonement. I believe with all my heart in this doctrine, but that is not what this co-worker needed. She simply needed to hear that Jesus died for her sins. All of that other information is secondary; it does not lead to salvation. And in this case, I am very much afraid it was getting in the way of salvation. We cannot understand the things of God until we have the Spirit of God.

Along with understanding, which is a gradual process, we receive righteousness, which is immediate. When we receive Christ, His righteousness is counted as our righteousness. That is why His sinless life was so important.

As sinful creatures, it is impossible for us to live the sinless life that God requires, so Christ did it for us. Then mysteriously, when God looks at our "sin account," He sees Christ's and sees no sin. It is as though we took a clean credit score and messed it all up. Instead of a perfect score of 850, we have reduced our score to 0. Whether through ignorance or greed, we have done everything wrong. Then Christ comes in and pays all of our debts and settles all of our accounts. And when God looks at our credit score, it's 850. Perfect. Okay, this analogy doesn't even come close really. A bad credit score in no way matches an entire life full of sin, but you get the point. If we would be grateful for a change in credit score, how much more grateful should we be for a change in the condition of our lives—from desperately sinful to perfectly righteous in God's eyes!

We are viewed as righteous, and we are also holy. This gets a little confusing, because we are told in Scripture that we are holy, and that we should work to be holy. In one sense, we are already holy—the moment we receive God's Holy Spirit, we are set apart from all of creation as one of God's chosen people. But in another sense, we must still strive to show that holiness in all of our daily activities. Can people look at your life and tell that God has set you apart for Himself? Do they see something different about you? A friend was telling me about a young girl she knows who was in tears one day because her friends were not as holy as she is. I think this young girl is missing the point. (Sort of like the man who won a medal for humility, only to have it taken away because he wore it.) Our holiness needs to be seen in our actions and in our words, but not by our proclaiming our holiness. The more we act in obedience to God's Word, the more others can see our holiness and desire it for themselves.

Please remember what holiness means—it is not "better than you." It is not sanctimonious, making a show of our piety. It is not judgmental of others. It is being set apart by God as His own and then choosing to obey God and His Word and to put Him in first place in our lives, in a quiet and humble manner. We can only begin in the smallest of ways to obey God in this life, but everyone who is born of God will begin to obey Him.

Holiness involves how we interact with all of God's creation. Regarding people, there is basically one rule and it is very simple: "Do to others what you would have them do to you." (Matthew 7:12) If everyone would just obey this one rule, the world would be a wonderful place. But of course we don't, so sometimes it isn't. Most major world religions have a version of this rule. In graduate school, I was assigned a paper on Jean Paul Sartre, an existentialist atheist philosopher and playwright. As Sartre thought about the world, even he came up with a version of this same rule. It just makes sense. Of course God thought of it first. Even more reason to follow it.

But how are we to treat the rest of creation? As just that—as something created by God. Man and woman's first job was to take care of creation. We are to preserve, conserve, and not waste what God has given us. We are to treat animals kindly, giving those in our care what they need to survive and thrive. If you choose a vegetarian lifestyle, that is your choice and I would support you in that choice, but let's not make the mistake of equating animals with human beings. God did give man and woman all kinds of animals as well as plants for food. He created man and woman differently from the way He created animals. Animals are wonderful creations, but they are not people.

Having created everything, God did not leave the world to take care of itself, but He is still involved in all of His creation. In fact, I understand from my scientific friends that when we consider the atom, everything in science would argue that the atom should fly apart. You and I should not exist. We should be in a billion tiny pieces. So what holds us together? God. Read Hebrews 1:3 again with that in mind. If God stopped for one minute, we would all literally fall apart. But we don't because God sustains and preserves us.

He also preserves us by providing for us. Some things He provides for everyone whether they believe in Him or not. Everyone is still held together. Everyone has food, shelter, clothing, etc. [Okay, most people.] But in some ways He particularly provides for His own people. There are special blessings that come from being a child of God. We know that He cares for us and will never leave us. We know that He is involved in our day to day activities and is concerned about the tiniest problems we might have. We know that He enjoys giving good gifts to those He loves. These are things reserved for His people. We also know that we will have an eternity with Him. Those who do not know Him have received their reward in full in this life. How sad that must be. This is it. This is all you get. This is the best it will ever be. There is only pain and suffering after this. In contrast, God's children know that pain and suffering is the temporary part, that this is worst it will ever be, and that after this, there is only joy and gladness.

Not only does God preserve us, He also governs us. Obviously, He has given us laws to live by, most notably the Ten Commandments. But He not only gives us laws to obey, He also guides and directs all of His creation. There are laws of physics that the entire universe follows. Where do you think those came from? Sometimes it seems that nature does a better job of obeying God than mankind does.

We must remember that God is always governing what happens on earth. We may not understand what's going on, but God always knows what is happening, and more importantly, He knows why it is happening. We should not be discouraged when things do not go the way we think they should, or when elections or politics fail to produce the results that we desire. We must always put our trust in God and not in man or in government. Human beings and human institutions will fail us and fall short of our expectations, but God will never fail us.

God has a perfect plan. We do not always [ever?] know exactly what that plan is. But God is always, let me repeat ALWAYS, in control of EVERYTHING. Things do not get out of His control. Whenever I feel that I don't understand what is happening in the world or in my life, I try to remember to be grateful that I have a God that I can't completely understand. That means that His wisdom and knowledge are so vastly superior to mine that He can know and understand things that I cannot begin to know and understand. So He is capable of knowing and understanding what is happening, and making it all turn out for the good of those who love Him.[8] God made you in His image in knowledge, righteousness, and holiness. He is preserving and governing all of your life. Take a moment to consider how that will affect your day to day living of that life from now on.

6

LESSON 6
WHO IS YOUR GOD?

Question 12: What special act of providence did God exercise toward man, in the estate in which he was created?

Answer: When God created man, He entered into a covenant of life with him, on condition of perfect obedience, forbidding him to eat of Tree of the Knowledge of Good and Evil, on the pain of death.

1. Genesis 2:17 gives us the penalty for breaking the covenant of life that God established with Adam and Eve. From what you read in that verse, what was the covenant of life that God made with Adam and Eve?
   Read Genesis 2:17

2. What was the one law that Adam and Eve were asked to obey to keep the covenant of life?
   Read Genesis 2:17

Question 13: Did our first parents continue in the estate in which they were created?

Answer: Our first parents, being left to the freedom of their own will, fell from the estate in which they were created, by sinning against God.

3. In the beginning, what was the only sin that Adam and Eve could possibly have committed?
   Read Genesis 2:17

Question 14: What is sin?

Answer: Sin is any lack of conformity to, or transgression of, the law of God.

4. How does a person sin by lack of conformity to the law of God?
   Read James 4:17

5. How does a person sin by transgression of the law of God?
   Read Daniel 9:11; Colossians 3:5

6. How have you sinned by lack of conformity to the law of God?

7. How have you sinned by transgression of the law of God?

Question: 15: What was the sin by which our first parents fell from the estate in which they were created.

Answer: The sin by which our first parents fell from the estate in which they were created was their eating of the forbidden fruit.

6. How did Eve quote the law that she and Adam had been given?
   Read Genesis 3:3

7. How did the serpent finally tempt Eve to eat the fruit?
   Read Genesis 3:4-5

8. What kind of fruit was it?
   Read Genesis 3:1-12

9. What does Scripture tell us about how Eve convinced Adam to eat the fruit?
   Read Genesis 3:6

10. What happened immediately after they ate the fruit?
    Read Genesis 3:7

LESSON 6
WHO IS YOUR GOD?

Catechism Questions 12, 13, 14, and 15

SUPPOSE IN ALL OF YOUR LIFE THERE WAS ONLY ONE LAW. NO TRAFFIC laws, no tax laws, no state laws, no federal laws—just one law: ***Don't Eat That***. You can eat anything else you want to. You can go anywhere you want to. You can do anything you want to. Just don't eat that one thing.

If you obey this one law, you will live in a perfect world forever. If you don't, you will die. Sounds like a good deal, doesn't it? I think I could live with that. The problem is, there would be that one thing, day after day, year after year. Always there. Staring at you. And you would start to wonder—what does it taste like? What does it feel like in your mouth? What is there about it that makes it so special? Why can't I have it?!

Have you ever been on a diet? All of a sudden, things you never even really wanted to eat seem incredibly important. I am thankful that I never started smoking because I'm not sure I would have the willpower to quit.

My husband once had a job teaching at a Christian college, and one part of his contract was that we both had to agree to two things: to attend a certain church and to not drink any alcohol, not even in our own home. The church was a good church and we didn't drink anyway, so we were not uncomfortable with signing this contract. But after a few months, those two stipulations became incredibly irritating. What if we wanted to go to a different church?! What right did they have to tell us what church to go to! And what if I wanted a glass of wine with dinner? I was an adult. How dare they tell us what to do in our own home! (Remember, we didn't have to sign that contract. He was free to refuse that job.)

So this is the situation Adam and Eve were faced with. One simple rule. One tree staring at them day after day, until Eve finally broke. We can understand it. We would have broken too. I can tell from what happened at that college that I certainly would have. But does that excuse her? Of course not. Because what her choice says about her is that she valued her own curiosity, her own "needs," above her love for God. She didn't love Him enough to obey one simple rule.

She had even added to the rule, possibly to help herself obey it. She had decided that she wouldn't even touch the tree, probably to keep herself from touching the fruit, to keep herself from eating the fruit. (God had never said not to touch the fruit, just not to eat it.) Now if that had helped Eve, I suppose it might have been okay. If something helps us avoid temptation, that can be a good thing. But we can't make those extra rules that we make for ourselves apply to everybody. Suppose Adam had touched the tree. Would she have yelled at him that he was breaking the rules? Jesus later on condemned the Pharisees for such behavior, for adding rules and regulations to the commands of God and then priding themselves on obeying their own rules rather than God's rules.[9]

So Eve's first problem was that she had really forgotten what the rule was. But her second problem was worse. She wanted to be like God. This was the temptation that got to her, the final straw. After she heard that, she could no longer resist. She took a bite; and she found that she did know something God knew. She knew what evil was. And not wanting to be alone in this knowledge, she gave some of the fruit to Adam. According to the passage in Genesis, it doesn't sound like he put up too much of a fight. There isn't any argument described there. She gave it to him and he ate it. So the deed was done.

As a side note, let's not blame the poor apple for this any longer. We are never told what kind of fruit this was. In my humble opinion, I think it was probably a fruit that we don't have any more. I do not know of any Knowledge of Good and Evil orchards around, so I suspect there are no such fruits anymore. You can picture that fruit any way you wish, but it did not look like anything you can get anywhere on earth today. I personally like apples and feel that they have suffered this indignity long enough.

But let's get back to this first sin—wanting to be like God. How is that manifest in our world today? How is it NOT manifest? There are some pretty blatant examples of this. Amazingly, there are people who have actually called themselves gods or Messiahs, such as David Koresh, who set himself up as the Messiah and leader of the Branch Davidians; Sun Myung Moon, the founder of the Unification Church, who sees his mission as completing what Christ left undone[10]; or the Maharishi Mahesh Yogi, the founder of Transcendental Meditation, who wanted to be seen as a Messiah.[11]

Then there are those who, though not calling themselves god, saw their role in society as that of a savior. Men like Napoleon, Adolf Hitler, Idi Amin, Pol Pot, and others have declared that they alone could save their nations from disaster. Ironically, all they managed to achieve was even greater disaster.

Even in our poetry, our wanting to be like God, or to be our own god, is evident. One of the most famous poems along this line is "Invictus" by William Ernest Henley, who died in 1903. The final stanza of that poem reads:

> It matters not how strait the gate,
> How charged with punishments the scroll,
> I am the master of my fate:
> I am the captain of my soul.

Interestingly, Timothy McVeigh, the man convicted of the Oklahoma City bombing, chose this poem to be his final statement. He gave a handwritten copy of it to the prison warden just before he was executed for his crime.

Does that surprise you? Horrify you? How could anyone claim that he is the captain of his own soul? Yet don't we all do that every single day?

Suppose I have a particularly difficult friend, and she has said something particularly difficult to me. I know I should respond in love, but it's been a long day, and I'm tired, and besides, she has done this one too many times. So I tell her what I really think. And I probably hurt her in the process. But putting that aside for the moment, what am I saying to God? Basically I have told Him that I know what He wants me to do, but I don't care. I am the captain of my ship, and I will make the decisions for my life.

Every time we sin, we are declaring ourselves to be our own god. We are saying, in effect, "I will make the rules this time, no matter what God or anyone else thinks." We may not be as blatant or as vocal about it as some have been, but we are just as guilty. That is why every sin is equal in the eyes of God. Every sin is rebellion against His authority; every sin is setting ourselves up as our own god.

There are basically two kinds of sins, or two kinds of rebellion, if you will. The first is to do what we are commanded not to do. This is what Adam and Eve did. They had only one rule, and they refused to obey it. They were told not to eat the fruit, and they ate it anyway. We all commit this kind of sin every day because we choose to do things we are told not to do. Probably not the big things. You have probably never murdered anyone in your life. You have probably never stolen anything—or have you? Have you ever "borrowed" supplies from work?

Anyway, we may not have committed sins that would send us to jail, but Jesus made it very clear that we can sin in thought as well as in action. In Matthew 5:21-22, He tells us that even being angry with our brother is a sin like murder. Further on, in verses 27-28, He says that to even think about committing adultery is a sin, even if we do not actually do the deed. So let's not be too quick to acquit ourselves of even the "big sins."

There is another kind of sin, and that is when we fail to do what we know we ought to do. Have you ever seen the bedroom of a teen-age girl? I have had three. Now there are admittedly exceptions to this, but most teen-age girls have mysteriously forgotten the use of a clothes hanger. Their floor is carpeted with the day's rejects, or with yesterday's latest fashion. Have you ever tried to get one of those girls to clean that mess up? Their response usually runs something like, "It's my room, so I should be allowed to live like I want to. Just close the door." (Ever say that to your mother?)

And we, in turn, reply with something truly profound, such as, "This is my house, and you will do as I say. When you get your own house you can live in any kind of mess you want to." (Honestly, is that the best we can come up with?)

We want the room clean because the disorder affects the entire family. But the disobedience affects the entire family as well. We want the rules of household obeyed. But what is the disobedience? The daughter didn't do something she was told not to do; she was in her room, minding her own business. However, she did not do something she was specifically told to do.

That is the second kind of sin. We know what we should do, but we are too lazy, or busy, or self-absorbed to do it. Who knows how many times that happens in a day, much less a lifetime. We can always make excuses and rationalize our choices, but in the end, the excuses are just that—excuses. Whenever there is a good act that should be done, and we don't do it, we have also told God that we are now in control. We are the captains of our own little ships, and we aren't interested in what He thinks.

So we are all sinful. We can blame Adam and Eve for letting sin into the world, but we know in our hearts that we would have done exactly what they did. And we still do it every day. We want to be in control of our own lives, to be our own gods. Fortunately, God works in spite of our attitudes and does not leave us to our own devices, mistakes, and failures. Even though we are so often unfaithful to Him, He is constantly faithful to us.

7

LESSON 7
WHERE DID WE GO WRONG?

Question 16: Did all mankind fall in Adam's first transgression?

Answer: ***The covenant being made with Adam, not only for himself, but for his descendants, all mankind, descending from him by ordinary generation, sinned in him and fell with him, in his first transgression.***

1. Who was included in the covenant of life that God made with Adam and Eve?
   Read I Corinthians 15:21-22; Romans 5:19

2. How did the results of the Fall apply to the descendants of Adam and Eve?
   Read Romans 5:12; Genesis 3:22

Question 17: Into what estate did the Fall bring mankind?
Answer: The Fall brought mankind into an estate of sin and misery.

3. How was all mankind affected by Adam and Eve's first sin?
   Read Romans 5:12; Genesis 3:16-19

Question 18: What is the sinfulness of that estate into which man fell?
Answer: The sinfulness of that estate into which man fell consists of: the guilt of Adam's first sin, the lack of original righteousness, and the corruption of his whole nature, which is commonly called original sin, together with all actual transgressions that proceed from it.

4. What does "original sin" mean?
   Read Psalm 14:2-3; Romans 3:23

5. What is the result of original sin?
   Read Matthew 15:19; Ephesians 2:1-3

Question 19: What is the misery of that estate into which man fell?

Answer: All mankind, by their fall, lost communion with God, are under His wrath and curse, and so made liable to all miseries of this life, to death itself, and to the pains of hell forever.

6. What does it mean to be under God's wrath and curse?
   Read Psalm 88:14-18

7. Why are the miseries of this life worse for those without God?
   Read Romans 1:18, 28-32; Philippians 4:6-7

8. What is different about death for the believer than for the unbeliever?
   Read Matthew 25:34, 41

9. How did Jesus describe Hell?
   Read Mark 9:48

10. Who was hell primarily created to punish? Where is the devil now?
    Read Matthew 25:41; I Peter 5:8; I John 4:4

LESSON 7
WHERE DID WE GO WRONG?
Catechism Questions 16, 17, 18, and 19

HAVE YOU EVER SIGNED A CONTRACT THAT INVOLVED YOUR ENTIRE family? Have you bought a house, opened a business, or borrowed money for any other reason? What would happen if you broke the contract? Would you be the only one affected? Unfortunately, the answer is usually no.

If a mother and father are unable to pay their mortgage or rent, the entire family is left without a place to live. If a small business goes bankrupt, often an entire family or several families are left without an income. What we do often affects others. Parents represent their children in paying the household bills. Business owners represent their employees in making business decisions. And so it was with Adam and Eve; they were our representatives in mankind's first dealings with God. I used to think that it was terribly unfair of God to punish everyone for the sins of these first two people, but now that I think about it logically, there was really no other choice.

What happened when Adam and Eve sinned? Evil entered the world. And along with evil came death. The first death recorded in the Bible was God's killing of an animal to make clothing for Adam and Eve. And since evil and death were in the world, obviously any children born to Adam and Eve would also be affected. They would know both good and evil, and they would be subject to death. There was no going back.

The punishment inflicted on Adam and Eve would also be inflicted on their children. Eve and all women who followed her would have pain in childbearing. If you have had a child, you know that this is no small thing. For some women, it is easier than others, but for every woman, there is pain involved. There is pain before the birth, during the birth, and even after the birth.

For Adam, and also for Eve, there was the difficulty of life on earth. Providing for our families would no longer be as easy as picking fruit off of trees. Adam and Eve, and all of their descendants, would have to work hard for their food. There would be drought, and floods, and insects, and harsh winds, and diseases that would destroy crops. None of this would have happened before the Fall.

Whatever problems you are facing today, you can blame them on Adam and Eve, at least a little. But not entirely, because much of the responsibility still falls on you. Although sin entered the world through Adam and Eve, we each choose to continue to sin on our own. If we are truly honest with ourselves, we will find that much of the misery and chaos in our lives is of our own making. We make choices based on our own selfish desires and find that they are not good for us at all. Some of the misery and chaos that we have to deal with is due to the choices of others. What we do affects others, and what they do affects us. All the way back to Adam and Eve. And on and on into the future.

Sounds pretty hopeless, doesn't it? And without Christ, it would be. Without Christ, this world wouldn't stand a chance. We would all just continue to sin and be sinned against as long as we were forced to live. That's basically what the term "original sin" means. Without Christ, we cannot do anything good. Without Christ, everyone sins. Everyone in the world is born with the tendency to sin.

But what about a sweet little newborn baby? She can't possibly sin, can she? She's so sweet and tiny and delicate. Just wait until that sweet little tiny baby is about four months old and then take something away from her that she wants. See how delicately she screams at you. Little babies can have a real temper! I know; I raised three girls. They were the three cutest little girls on the planet at the time, but they were still sinful little creatures.

My friend Cara's second child was a darling little boy. One morning when he was six weeks old, she put him in his car seat to go to the grocery store. He screamed. Cara knew something must be terribly wrong, so she took him out to see what was the matter. She checked his diaper, burped him, rearranged his clothing, and everything seemed fine. He seemed happy. She put him back in the car seat and he screamed again. So she took him out and checked him over, and again he seemed fine. She put him back in the car seat, and you guessed it, he screamed. Cara finally realized that she had a very smart little baby boy. At the age of six weeks, he had figured out how to get out of that car seat—scream really loud. Now I don't know if that's exactly sinful, but it is at least manipulative. And that was at six weeks old.

We humans are sinful. We are born sinful. And we continue to be sinful for our entire lives. That is original sin. We cannot change it. Actually, we don't want to change it. We are very happy with our sin. We are not always happy with the consequences, but we like doing what we want and thinking of our needs and desires first. We don't want to think about God, and we don't want to try to please Him. We don't even much like the idea of God at all. Left to ourselves, apart from His grace, we pretty much reject Him altogether.

And when we reject Him, we have no relationship with Him. We don't want one, so we don't think we miss it; but there is something in everyone that yearns for God. Deep in our hearts, everyone knows that there is a God who created him or her. When they are facing real trouble, they want God to be there. How many people all of a sudden began to pray on September 11, 2001?

But Christ does not want lukewarm believers.[12] We cannot love Him only when it suits us. Either believe or don't believe, but there is no middle ground. If we do not truly believe, then we are under His wrath and curse. So when we are afraid, there is really no one to turn to; we are alone with our fears.

Scripture even tells us that if we persist in our unbelief, God will give us over to our sins.[13] God will leave us alone to suffer the full brunt of the consequences of what we are doing. If we truly desire a life of sin, then He will allow us to live that life, with everything that it entails. He will allow us to have what we think we want. He will allow us to associate with the type of people who also want that lifestyle. He will not intervene to make our life easier. There will be sin in all of its debauchery and wickedness, with all of its accompanying misery. We will be not only the perpetrators but also the victims of a totally sinful lifestyle.

Contrast that with the promises made to those who trust in God. In our salvation, Christ, rather than Adam, becomes our representative with God. He promises to be near to us always, and to hear us when we call. He tells us to cast our cares on Him, and He promises to give us peace even in the midst of frightening circumstances because He will never leave us. And not only that, when this life is over, He promises us a place in His eternal kingdom forever.

What is the promise for those who continue to reject God? There is a promise for them as well, but it's not very attractive. God promises that they will be cast into the lake of fire, or Hell.

I don't like writing about Hell, and I'm pretty sure you don't like reading about it. In fact, I would prefer to skip this part of the lesson completely. But if Jesus talked about it, I don't have the liberty of ignoring it. Jesus warned against Hell, describing it as a place where the worm never dies and the fire is not quenched. It is a terrible place. And it is real. It is not something someone in church made up to scare people into coming forward and getting saved. Jesus warned people about it to scare them into taking their relationship with God seriously. And if it causes some people to recognize their need for a Savior and accept God's plan of salvation, then I have no problem with it.

I want to put to rest a myth about Hell that has circulated for years, perhaps for centuries. Maybe you could call this a "pet peeve" of mine, but I have heard so many people, even some preachers, get this wrong, and so many Christian songs get this wrong, that it is really starting to bother me. So let's set the record straight right now—Satan is not in charge of Hell. Hell is a place that God created to punish Satan and his followers. God is in charge of Hell, not Satan. Satan is not in Hell now; He is on earth, roaming around, creating havoc, tempting people to sin, causing destruction, etc. Satan will have no control over Hell, and it is not somewhere that he wants to be. I don't know where we got the idea that Satan is the King of Hell, except perhaps from Satan himself. The idea is nowhere in Scripture. Satan is referred to as the prince of the power of the air or the prince of this world, which confirm the idea that He is on earth seeking people to do his bidding. Hell is a real place, and it is terrifying. We don't want to be there and neither does Satan.

So far this is a pretty depressing picture; man without God is hopeless, doomed to a life of sin and misery on earth and an eternity in the lake of fire. Thankfully, the picture isn't finished. In the next lesson we will get to see things from a happier vantage point, our redemption in Christ.

8

LESSON 8
WHO IS THIS MAN?

Question 20: Did God leave all mankind to perish in the estate of sin and misery?

Answer: God, having out of his mere good pleasure, from all eternity, elected some to everlasting life, did enter into a covenant of grace, to deliver them out of the estate of sin and misery, and to bring them into an estate of salvation by a Redeemer.

1. When did God decide on His plan of salvation?
   Read Ephesians 1:4

2. Why did God elect some people to everlasting life?
   Read Ephesians 1:4-5

3. Why do people need a Redeemer?
   Read Psalm 143:2; Romans 3:11-12

4. Why do you personally need a Redeemer?

5. Romans 3:23 and I Corinthians 15 15:3-4 describe what is called the Covenant of Grace. From what you read in these verses, what is the covenant of grace?
   Read Romans3:23; I Corinthians 15:3-4

Question 21: Who is the Redeemer of God's elect?

Answer: The only Redeemer of God's elect is the Lord Jesus Christ, who, being the eternal Son of God, became man, and so was, and continues to be, God and man, in two distinct natures, and one Person forever.

6. When did Christ begin to exist?
   Read John 1:1, 17:5

7. What does it mean that Christ is the Son of God?
   Read John 3:16; John 10:30; Matthew 3:17

Question 22: How did Christ, being the Son of God, become man?

Answer: ***Christ, the Son of God, became man, by taking to Himself a true body, and a reasonable soul, being conceived by the power of the Holy Spirit, in the womb of the Virgin Mary, and born of her, yet without sin.***

8. How was Jesus conceived?
   Read Luke 1:35

9. Why is the virgin birth important?
   Read Isaiah 7:14; Luke 1:35

10. How do we know that Christ had a real body, that he was fully man?
    Read Luke 2:25-28, 8:45, 15:2, 22:63, 23:46

11. How do we know that Christ was really God?
    Read Mark 2:10, 4:39, 5:35-42, 6:48, 16:1-7

12. Why is Christ's sinless life important?
    Read Hebrews 4:15; Romans 5:19

LESSON 8
WHO IS THIS MAN?
Catechism Questions 20, 21, and 22

I MENTIONED IN AN EARLIER LESSON THAT MY HUSBAND AND I TAUGHT a class for young children. He used to explain the problem of sin to them in this way: "We like to go outside and play, and sometimes we get really dirty. So then our mothers make us go in and take a bath and wash all the dirt off. They don't want us getting the dirt on the sofa or even the carpet, so they are happier when we are all clean. Sin is like invisible dirt. When we do something wrong, then we get invisible sin dirt on us. We can't see it, but God can. But we can't wash off the sin dirt with soap and water. We could scrub and scrub, but we could never get it off. But God's heaven is a holy place, and He can't let anyone in if they have sin dirt on them. So He sent Jesus to die for us. Jesus died to pay the penalty for our sins. Then when we believe in Jesus, all that sin dirt just goes away. It is washed off by Jesus. We can't wash it off, but Jesus can."

Admittedly, this is very simplistic, but we were working with three- and four-year-olds. But they got the message. One mother told me that her son was watching television when a commercial came on for laundry detergent. He piped up and said, "That stuff can't wash off sin dirt." How exciting! He was only four, but he got it.

We all have "sin dirt." And we can't get rid of it. But for some inexplicable reason, God wants us in His heaven, and He wants fellowship with us while we are still on earth. You know, there are days when I am in such a bad mood, I don't even want fellowship with myself, but God still cares for me and wants to be with me. God likes me better than I like myself.

God knew before He created the universe that we would have this problem. Long before He created them, He knew that Adam and Eve would sin, and He had a plan to fix things. The Bible simply tells us that He did this for His purposes. Remember, the mind of God is vastly superior to ours, so we just have to accept that and let it be.

We do have some obligations, however. We are told to walk in good works and to treat others as we would want to be treated, etc. But that is not why God chose to save us. He didn't need this world or anything in it. He didn't look at the future and say, "There are going to be some real problems there that I am not going to be able to handle by myself, so I guess I'll have to save some people so they can help me straighten things up." He could have wiped out the whole place the moment Adam and Eve took that first bite of fruit, but for His own purposes, He didn't.

Adam and Eve, and therefore all of the rest of us, broke the Covenant of Life, which is also sometimes called the Covenant of Works. We all sin. No one is righteous or seeks God on his or her own. So God instituted what we call the Covenant of Grace. Basically, that is the Gospel. Since we needed a Savior, God provided one—Himself, in the form of God the Son.

God the Son, Christ, has always existed. He did not begin to exist when He was born in that stable. He was part of the Trinity that created the universe and that created you. He was part of the Trinity that created the plan of salvation. Christ created the men who would crucify Him and the tree that would provide the wood for His cross. He was totally and intimately involved with the plan of salvation. Of course, He was obeying His Father, but He also created the instructions.

That does not mean that the instructions were not unpleasant. Christ was also fully man. He suffered just as we suffer. It is important that we understand what the Bible teaches us about Christ's birth as well as His death. The Bible is a unit. We are not allowed to pick and choose what to believe. I have well-meaning friends who have said that they believe in the resurrection, but they don't think the Virgin Birth is really all that important. They can believe in Christ without having to believe in the Virgin Birth. But can they really? Can they fully understand and accept all that Christ is and all that He has done without acknowledging His miraculous birth?

First of all, the Virgin Birth was one of the signs given to us by God that would confirm the coming of the Messiah. Isaiah prophesied roughly 600 years before Christ's birth that He would be born of a virgin and born in Bethlehem. Refusing to believe in the Virgin Birth is refusing to acknowledge the prophecy and confirmation regarding Christ that God has given us.

Second, the Virgin Birth seems to me to have been necessary for Christ to have lived the sinless life that He did. Now this is just my opinion, but in my field of study, the use of logic is critical. I teach logical reasoning in most of my classes. Now, I don't believe that our sin nature is in our DNA. If scientists are able to figure out what every single part of our DNA is for, I don't think they will find a sin part. In my opinion, our inheritance of sin is spiritual, not physical. But my argument is this:

- The only way to live a sinless life is to avoid inheriting the sinfulness of Adam and Eve.
- In order to avoid inheriting that sinfulness, a person would have to have a sinless parent.
- The only sinless being in the universe is God Himself.
- Therefore, in order to live a sinless life, God Himself would have to be your parent.

BINGO. That is exactly what happened. Christ had a completely human mother, but a completely perfect Father. Therefore, He could live a sinless life. In order for Christ to be both fully human and fully divine, He would have to have a fully human parent and a fully divine parent. And that's what He had.

Now I don't think for one minute that God is bound by my finite logic. I know that God can do anything He chooses to do. I do, however, believe that God created the logic that we use, and that in this case, it fits the situation.

There are those who argue that in order for Christ to live a sinless life, His mother had to be sinless as well. They believe therefore that Mary was somehow sinless. That will get you quickly to a logical quagmire. Because if Mary had to be sinless in order for Jesus to be sinless, then both of her parents would have had to be sinless in order for Mary to be sinless, and all four of her grandparents would have had to be sinless in order for her parents to be sinless, etc., etc. You see the problem. And if you argue that God somehow worked a miracle and made Mary sinless, then why not start with Jesus instead of Mary? I do believe that Mary deserves our honor and respect, because she was highly favored by God in being chosen to be the mother of the Messiah. However, I do not believe that she was anything more than a godly young woman who was chosen to carry out a difficult yet highly honorable task for the glory of God.

So what does this all mean for us anyway? Why does it matter that Christ was sinless? So what if He did sin? Only that if Christ did sin, then we are no better off than if He had never come to earth at all. Christ died to pay for our sins. He had to be sinless for his death to conform to God's law. We'll talk about that in the next lesson. But let's put that aside for a moment. There is still another reason we needed Him to live a sinless life. Once the debt is wiped clean, paid, what is in its place? If that is it, then it's as though we never existed. No debt, no sin, no life. You see, not only did Christ die for us, He also lived for us. He suffered every temptation that we do[14], and sometimes to a greater degree. Scripture tells us that He spent forty days in the wilderness without food, and then He was tempted by Satan. How many of us have gone forty days without eating?

And although Christ was tempted in every way that we are, He never sinned. Not once. Not even as a child. No wonder He had problems with His brothers.[15] What would it be like growing up with a perfect brother? Some of you may have been compared unfavorably with a sibling and felt that they were treated as though they were perfect. But what if they really were perfect? And what about Mary and Joseph? What would it be like to raise a truly perfect child—a child whom you knew was really God? Can you imagine what you would do if anyone complained to you about Him?

Neighbor: Something is missing from my shop, and I saw your son Jesus around there right before I noticed it was gone.
Joseph: Well I know he couldn't have taken it because…[he's God!—they'll think I'm crazy!] …well, I just know it wasn't him.
Neighbor: Well, you just keep an eye on him. He's too good. That kind of kid is always up to something.

Notice in Scripture how slow those closest to Him were in believing in Him.[16] They had seen His perfection, and maybe it was just too much for them.

But it's not too much for us; in fact, it makes all the difference for us for all eternity because Jesus' perfect life is credited to us. We have to have lived a life.

We have to have a record. So when we accept Christ, God counts His record as our record. Our own record no longer exists; our sins are all forgiven, and it is as though we ourselves have lived Jesus' sinless life. This is the only way we can enter into God's kingdom. We cannot earn our own way in. We can't get rid of our own "sin dirt." We can't make ourselves clean enough or righteous enough to present ourselves to God. But Christ can, and He did. Thanks be to God for His indescribable gift!

9

LESSON 9
WHAT DOES CHRIST DO?

Question 23: What offices does Christ execute as our Redeemer?

Answer: Christ, as our Redeemer, executes the offices of a prophet, of a priest, and of a king, both in His estate of humiliation and exaltation.

Question 24: How does Christ execute the office of a prophet?

Answer: Christ executes the office of a prophet in revealing to us, by His Word and Spirit, the will of God for our salvation.

1. What is the job of a prophet?
   Read Deuteronomy 18:18

2. What does Christ reveal to us by His Word?
   Read Psalm 119:11, 42, 49, 68 104

3. How does Christ reveal things to us by His Spirit?
   Read John 14:26; Luke 12:12

Question: How does Christ execute the office of a priest?

Answer: Christ executes the office of a priest in his once offering up of Himself a sacrifice to satisfy divine justice, and reconcile us to God, and in making continual intercession for us.

4. What is the job of a priest?
   Read Leviticus 1:5, I Samuel 12:19

5. What was the purpose of the Old Testament sacrificial system?
   Read Leviticus 6:7; 16:30

6. What was the requirement for an animal used as an atonement sacrifice?
   Read Leviticus 9:3

7. How did Christ serve as a sacrifice for us?
   Read I Peter 1:18-19

8. How does Christ make intercession for us?
   Read Hebrews 7:24-25; John 17:20-26

Question 26: How does Christ execute the office of a king?

Answer:* *Christ executes the office of a king in subduing us to Himself, in ruling and defending us, and in restraining and conquering all His and our enemies.

9. What is the job of a king?
   Read I Samuel 8:20; Proverbs 8:15, 20:26

10. How does Christ subdue and rule over us?
    Read Romans 8:9

11. How does He defend us?
    Read Psalm 10:17-18; Romans 5:9

12. How does He restrain and conquer His and our enemies?
    Read Romans 12:19-20; Proverbs 14:14; Matthew 25:31-33, 41

LESSON 9
WHAT DOES CHRIST DO?
Questions 23, 24, 25, and 26

IF THERE IS ONE THING THAT I AM NOT, IT IS A PROPHET, AT LEAST IN the sense of telling the future. I have absolutely no sense of what is likely to happen. In fact, the more sure I am that something is going to happen, the more likely it seems to be that it will not happen. So if there is a gift of prophecy, I definitely haven't got it. The word prophet, or prophecy, has another meaning in the Bible, though; it can also mean a teacher, or one who speaks the Word of God to others. It is in this sense that we will consider Jesus as a prophet, although I'm pretty sure He can predict the future, too.

What better teacher can we have than Jesus? Who better to explain God to us than God Himself? Who better to show us what God is like? Although that was not Jesus' primary purpose for coming to earth, it was certainly a wonderful benefit. The slogan "What Would Jesus Do" has taken a bad rap, because it's a really good question. When we are faced with a dilemma, what better example could we follow? Of course, the only way to know what Jesus would really do is to be thoroughly familiar with what Jesus actually did.

It is a serious mistake to be vaguely aware of the kind of person Jesus was and then imagine what we think He might have done in a given situation. For example, if we are only aware of Jesus as a God of love, we can assume that He would tolerate any and all types of misbehavior. But when we know about His anger at the moneylenders in the Temple, we know that His compassion did not extend to everyone and everything. Jesus did not tolerate those who were defiling the holiness of the Temple. His anger at the Pharisees, the teachers of the law, shows us that he expected those who knew better to do better. He did expect people to behave according to His standards. We need to study the Scriptures to know who Jesus was before we can be confident in knowing what He would do.

We also need to study the Scriptures to read what others have said about Him and what they have to teach us. The entire Bible is the Word of God, and it is the primary way that Jesus teaches us today. The more familiar we are with the teachings of the Bible, the less susceptible we will be to false teachings when we are confronted with them.

I have been told that the way government agencies train people to detect counterfeit money is simply to have them handle real money over and over and over. Then when they come into contact with the counterfeit stuff, it just doesn't feel right. Because they know the real thing so well, they are immediately alert to the fake. I don't know if this is true or not, but it makes my point. That is how it should be with the truths of the Bible. We should be so familiar with the real thing that we are automatically on alert when something doesn't sound right.

And fortunately, we don't have to depend on our own weak memories. (Mine is going by the second.) The Holy Spirit is here to guide us and to help us understand what we learn and to remember it in the future. Without the Holy Spirit, none of the truths of God's Word would make any sense to us anyway, because they are spiritually discerned. To those without the Spirit, as I have said before, these truths can seem as nonsense, or they can seem offensive. We need to remember this for ourselves and for our friends and family who need to believe. First, they need Christ and His Spirit. Otherwise, they cannot understand anything else.

Not only is Jesus our prophet, but He is our priest—and also our sacrifice. In Old Testament times, people sinned just as we do now. They needed a way to atone for their sins, a visible, tangible way that they could see, hear, smell, and feel. So God instituted the sacrificial system. When they sinned, either knowingly or unknowingly (after they figured it out), they were to bring a certain type of sacrifice, and the priest was to burn some or all of it on the altar to atone for the person's sins. The reason I am so vague about the instructions, is that there are so many of them for so many different types of sacrifices. Anyway, if the sacrifice was to be an animal, it was to be an animal without a blemish or imperfection of any kind.

Once a year, the high priest would offer a sacrifice of atonement for his sins and the sins of the nation. At that time, and only at that time, he could enter the section of the Temple behind the veil called the Holy of Holies, where the Ark of the Covenant was kept. He would sprinkle some of the blood of the sacrifice on the Ark as atonement for the sins of the people. This was a major day in the life of the nation of Israel, and it had to occur every year. The blood of an animal is not sufficient to pay for the sins of the people once and for all time.

But the blood of Christ is sufficient. The sacrificial system of the Old Testament merely pointed the way to the sacrifice of Christ. In the previous lesson, we talked about the necessity of Christ's living a sinless life. He had to be sinless to be a sacrifice without blemish, which was required by the law of God. He had to be God for His sacrifice to be big enough to pay for all of our sins. But thanks be to God, it was enough. Since Christ paid for our sins, once and for all time, we no longer need to offer a yearly animal sacrifice. It is finished.

So Christ is the priest and also the sacrifice. As the sacrifice, He has completed the job. Our sins are paid for. As the priest, He continues His work. But Christ is no ordinary priest. First of all, He did not fit the earthly requirements for a Hebrew priest because He was not a descendant of Levi. He is specially ordained for this task.[17] On earth, He acted as a priest by teaching the people the truths of God's Word, and by interceding for them in prayer. He also performed the final sacrifice. Earthly priests could enter the Holy of Holies only once a year, and they brought the blood of an animal to pay for their own sins as well as the sins of the people. Christ is forever in the Holy place, of which the Holy of Holies was just a shadow,[18] and He has brought His own perfect blood. He had no sins of His own, so His blood is the complete and perfect sacrifice for everyone who will believe in Him. And in that Holy place, He still intercedes for us today. He applies His sacrifice to each of us as payment for our sins. He prays for us with God the Father. He will continue as our priest forever.

And speaking of the kingdom, who do you suppose is the king? Silly question. Jesus, of course. We have all heard, and perhaps sung, the famous "Hallelujah Chorus" in the *Messiah*, by Handel. There is something beyond awe-inspiring about singing the words "King of kings and Lord of lords."

This past December, I was privileged to be a part of a church choir that performed a segment of that chorus during our annual Christmas concert. The following Sunday, we decided that rather than concluding the service with the traditional "Amen," we would end with the "King of kings" part of the *Messiah*. The pastor did not know this. However, his sermon was about the Kingship of Christ. He talked about references to the Kingship of Christ in the Scripture passages that deal with Christ's birth. He spoke of the numerous Christmas hymns that mention the Kingship of Christ. He then concluded with a call to make Christ the King of your own life. Those of us in the choir were on the edge of our seats. We couldn't wait to sing that chorus! Those words have never been more meaningful to me. I'm sure the congregation thought that we had put that all together on purpose, but we knew who had really put it together—it was all God.

When we went back to the choir room, we were all talking about the amazing thing that had just happened, until one of the choir members asked, "Why are we always so surprised when God does something wonderful?"

I don't know. Why were we so surprised? We had such joy that morning. Don't you think God enjoyed it too? He is the King, after all. He controls everything, even our morning worship service. He promises to be there even when two or three are gathered in His name, so why are we shocked when He shows up in a really tangible way?

We should want to know He's there. We call on Him in time of need, so shouldn't we be glad He's there in other times as well? As our King, Christ is our defender, and as such, He watches over us and is intimately involved in our lives. He promises to protect us, and in particular, to protect us from the wrath of God. We are not promised freedom from trouble; in fact, we are promised that as believers, we will have trouble. But we are promised that we will not have to go through that trouble alone. Even our greatest enemy Satan cannot stand against the name of Jesus Christ.

For a moment, I want to address the issue of those who do not acknowledge Christ. How does He deal with them? First, He tells us that He will deal with them, and that we are not to seek our own vengeance. In fact, we are to repay evil with good. That is very difficult to do; actually, without Christ, it is probably impossible. It can seem pretty close to impossible sometimes even with Christ. Second, we know that in eternity, they will receive their punishment. Jesus painted a very bleak picture for those who deny Him, or for those who act in His name without serving the God He really is.

For me, another sad part of the picture is painted in Matthew 6:2. Basically, Jesus is warning here not to behave like the Pharisees, who did things for the praise of men, because they have received their reward in full. So what I understand from this passage is that if your goal in this life is praise from men, or lots of money, or something else in this world, you may get it; but that will be all you get. There will be nothing else. It is sort of like the person whose best years were in high school and everything else is downhill from there. I feel sorry for those folks. Only this is much worse. Jesus will give these people what they want. For a few years, a very short time considering the length of eternity, they will have fame, or money, or whatever. Then it will be over. But instead of nothing, they will have punishment and an eternity of regret. They will have received their reward in full.

But for those who trust in Christ, our reward is still to come. We live in expectation of reigning with Christ in glory. In the meantime, while we wait here on earth, Christ is always with us. As our prophet, He continues to teach us the truths about Himself. As our priest, He intercedes for us in the Holiest of holy places, heaven itself. And as our king, He rules over us and defends us against all of our enemies, even Satan himself.

10

LESSON 10
THE WORST THING, OR THE BEST THING?

Question 27: What was Christ's humiliation?

Answer: ***Christ's humiliation consisted in His being born, and that in a low condition, made under the law, undergoing the miseries of this life, the wrath of God, and the cursed death of the cross, in being buried, and continuing under the power of death for a time.***

1. In what ways was Christ's birth a humiliation for Him?
   Read Philippians 2:6-7; Luke 2:7

2. How did Christ undergo the miseries of this life?
   Read Hebrews 2:18; Matthew 8:20; Philippians 2:8

3. How did Christ undergo the wrath of God?
   Read Matthew 27:45-50

4. In what way was Christ's burial a humiliation?
   Read Matthew 27:57-61

Question 28: What is Christ's exaltation?

Answer: Christ's exaltation consists in His rising again from the dead on the third day, in ascending into heaven, in sitting at the right hand of God the Father, and in coming to judge the world at the last day.

5. What is remarkable about Christ's resurrection?
   Read 2 Timothy 1:10; Hebrews 2:14; I Corinthians 6:14

6. Describe Christ's ascension into Heaven.
   Read Acts 1:9

7. What is significant about Christ's being seated at the right hand of God the Father?
   Read I Peter 3:22

8. What will be the signs of Christ's return?
   Read Matthew 24:29-31; I Thessalonians 4:16-17

Question 29: How do we take part in the redemption purchased by Christ?

Answer: We take part in the redemption purchased by Christ by the effectual application of it to us by His Holy Spirit.

9. Why can we not achieve redemption, or salvation, on our own?
   Read Romans 3:10-11, 23

10. How do we receive salvation?
    Read Romans 10:9

Question 30: How does the Spirit apply to us the redemption purchased by Christ?

Answer: The Spirit applies to us the redemption purchased by Christ by working faith in us, and thereby uniting us to Christ in our effectual calling.

11. Where does the faith to believe in Christ come from?
    Read Ephesians 2:8

LESSON 10
THE WORST THING, OR THE BEST THING?
Catechism Questions 27 and 28

A FEW YEARS AGO LAEL WAS ASKED TO TAKE PART IN A FRIEND'S WEDDING as an honorary bridesmaid. The bride already had quite a few bridesmaids, so three girls were asked to participate but not to stand in the front with the rest of the party. Lael was flattered to be asked because she had only known the bride a relatively short amount of time. In fact, she met the bride's parents only a few days before the wedding. When the big day came, everything was absolutely perfect. The couple was gorgeous, the day was beautiful, and everyone was thrilled! The father of the bride announced each member of the wedding party as they walked into the reception hall. When Lael's turn came, he called out the wrong name. She was really, really embarrassed! She just wanted to be known for who she was. I suppose she thought that by being called the wrong name, others would assume that the father didn't know her, and it felt embarrassing not to be known. I think we have all been in situations where we are mistaken for another person or where someone does not recognize us, even when we know who she is.

Now take that embarrassment and multiply it by a million. That was the humiliation Christ suffered for us. Here He is, the King of the Universe, the Creator of every being that He meets, and they have no idea who He is. Not only that, but He is now subject to the laws He set and the people He put in place to govern! His strength is weakened; He has gone from being an all-powerful God to having human strength. He was born in a stable among the animals, the lowliest place He could have been born. He is also subject to temptation and is tested in extreme circumstances, such as fasting in the desert for 40 days and then being tempted with food. He knew where He came from and He knew what He had given up. But for His own purposes, He suffered all this humiliation and in the end died a cruel death because it was the only way we could be saved. I have read a little about death on a cross, and I know that it is one of the most painful and slow ways to die.

But Christ suffered something even more painful than death; He suffered the wrath of God. The Bible tells us that God forsook Jesus while He took on our sins on the cross. In that sense, it was like Jesus was torn from Himself. The triune God—Father, Son, and Holy Spirit—have always had perfect unity and perfect communication. God has always existed and will always exist in those three persons. The Trinity has never been broken, except for that one time.

This is monumental. Forever, for the entire span of eternity, God has existed and will continue to exist in perfect harmony, in perfect communion, in perfect communication—except for that one small period of about three hours. Christ took on the sins of all those He came to save, and God the Father turned away. The Trinity was broken. There was no more communication between the Father and the Son. There was no more harmony. I can't even find the words to stress the significance of this moment in history. It is as if God Himself were torn apart.

No wonder there were signs of this on earth. The moment this happened, light became darkness. We know what was happening because Jesus cried out, "My God, my God, why have you forsaken me!" He did not call out "My Father." The relationship was broken. He called Him "God." And then Jesus suffered alone. Totally alone. He had been forsaken by His friends and finally by His Father. And He did this for us.

And when He had suffered enough, when the penalty was paid, He gave up His spirit. Again, notice what Scripture tells us. Jesus' life was not taken from Him; He gave it up.[19] He chose when to die—when He had accomplished what He had come to earth to do. And what He had done was to open the doors of heaven to all who would believe in Him. Once again, the earth responded: an earthquake shook the ground and rocks broke in two. More importantly, the curtain of the temple covering the Holy of Holies, where the high priest met with God, was torn in two. The curtain that separated the mercy seat of God from the people was ripped apart, giving access to the throne of God to anyone who believes. That veil was removed by Jesus; through Him we can now approach the throne of grace with confidence that our sins are forgiven.

But even after Jesus' death, He suffered one last humiliation. He did not receive a funeral or even a proper burial. He was taken away and buried in secret. No one mourned publicly; no one gave a eulogy on his behalf.

But three days later...oh the glory! I have often wondered what happened when Jesus conquered death and came back to life. I wonder what we would have seen in that grave before the angels or Mary saw Him. How awesome that would have been! But even though we did not see it, we receive the benefits from His resurrection, because as Christ rose, so will we. It is because of his death on the cross and resurrection that we can be accepted into heaven; there was no other way for us to be saved.

Jesus stayed on earth for only a short time before He ascended into heaven. I also like to picture this: the disciples watch as Jesus ascends into the sky like a rocket until they can't see anything but a dot. I wonder what they were thinking.... Finally, Jesus receives the glory that was all His to begin with! He receives the highest honor from God the Father and is placed at His right hand. Not only that, but He is returned to His position as Ruler of all creation. Praise God!

We can also look forward to Christ's coming again. The Bible tells us that Christ's return will be nothing like His first coming. This time it will be like one of those dramatic scenes from a sci-fi or epic movie. The whole sky will grow dark and Christ will ride in with His power and glory. A trumpet will sound and those who are dead in Christ will be raised, and the living also will be taken up with Him. He will never again suffer the humiliation He suffered the first time. He will finally be recognized; the Scripture says that every knee will bow and every tongue will confess that He is Lord.[20]

My friend Jeff had a professor in college who was extremely antagonistic towards the Christian faith. Day after day Jeff had to listen to this professor criticize Christians or the church or the Bible. One day he had had enough. The professor said something like, "When I die, I'm going to get in God's face and ask him why he didn't do something about some of the problems we have down here." Jeff spoke up boldly and said, "No, you won't. You will get down on your knees and worship your Creator." You see, in the end, everyone will realize who Christ is—who God is. But for many, it will be too late. Even though they will finally acknowledge God, they will not be allowed to spend eternity with Him. There won't be any second chances.

Lael says that she sometimes dreams about the day when Christ is finally known to the world for who He truly is. She has talked to so many people who don't care or don't want to have anything to do with Jesus. Even saying that name causes them embarrassment or anger. Just the name! Our hearts long that they know the truth, and we pray they do before it is too late.

11

LESSON 11
HIDE AND SEEK, OR HIDE AND FIND?

Question 31: What is effectual calling?

Answer: ***Effectual calling is the work of God's Spirit, by which, convincing us of our sin and misery, enlightening our minds in the knowledge of Christ, and renewing our wills, he persuades and enables us to embrace Jesus Christ, freely offered to us in the Gospel.***

1. How does the Holy Spirit convince us of our sin?
   Read John 16:7-8; Romans 3:20

2. How does the Holy Spirit enable us to embrace Jesus Christ?
   Read 2 Corinthians 5:17; I Peter 1:23

3. Can we understand the knowledge of Christ without the renewing of our minds by the Holy Spirit?
   Read I Corinthians 2:14

4. Are only those people saved who are effectually called?
   Read John 6:44

5. Is it possible for a person to want to be saved, but not be effectually called?
   Read Jeremiah 29:13; John 6:37

6. What is the last point in a person's life that he or she may receive Christ?
   Read Luke 23:39-43

7. Is salvation the work of an individual, or the work of God?
   Read Ephesians 2:1, 4-5, 8-9

8. When did God decide who would be effectually called?
   Read 2 Thessalonians 2:13-14; 2 Timothy 1:9

9. Why did God effectually call us?
   Read 2 Timothy 1:9; Ephesians 1:4

10. Why is it not unfair of God to punish those who reject Him? Read Romans 1:19-21

11. If salvation is the work of God, why do we need evangelism? Read Romans 10:14; Matthew 28:19

LESSON 11
HIDE AND SEEK, OR HIDE AND FIND?
Catechism Questions 29, 30, and 31

HAVE YOU EVER PLAYED HIDE-AND-SEEK? WHEN MY SIBLINGS AND I WERE younger, we used to love to play Sardines with our cousins. Sardines is a version of hide-and-seek where one person hides and everyone else is "It." Except when you find the person who is hiding, you hide with him. The last person to find the rest of the group "loses" and hides first next time. But we added a little twist to the game, and we played it in the dark. Somehow we managed to convince our parents to stay confined to the kitchen while the seven to ten of us cousins had free rein in a dark house, hiding in all kinds of strange and unusual places. I cannot imagine what my mother was thinking to allow us to do that!

Those are good memories. Sardines, hide-and-seek—those childish games were fun. But in a way, everyone on earth is playing a game of cosmic hide-and-seek, and the "It" they are trying to hide from is God. And while in the child's game, we want to be found, in this cosmic game, we desperately do not. Throughout Scripture, we are told that no one seeks God; no one does good. We run from God and we reject His salvation.

The plan of salvation is very simple. All we have to do is believe in the Lord Jesus Christ and we will be saved. But to do that would mean to submit to Him, to acknowledge and repent of our sins, and to be willing to live for Him. And no one wants to do that. Have you ever talked to someone before she was ready to give her life to Christ? She will offer up every excuse in the world as to why she cannot possibly commit herself to Christ. A former pastor called this hiding behind bushes. If a person is "hiding behind bushes," and you manage to defeat one of her arguments, and thus pull up her bush, she will just run around till she finds another one to hide behind. You cannot argue someone into the kingdom of God if she is not ready to hear the Gospel.

If God left it up to us to choose Him, His heaven would be empty. People basically do not want to choose God. So God chooses us. The Holy Spirit comes to us and convicts us of our sin and our need for a Savior, while at the same time giving us the faith that we need to believe in Christ. We are made into a new creation, one that can now understand the things of God. This is all totally a work of God, something we cannot possibly understand. It is, in every sense of the word, a mystery. How God does this is more than our finite minds can comprehend. Nor can we comprehend why He does this; it is simply for His own purposes. Those who have been called by God need to thank Him continually for this incomprehensible gift. We do not know why we have been called; we only know that we have been changed and that our lives are now His. We should also realize that there is nothing that we have contributed to our salvation. Our salvation is, from beginning to end, the work of God.

And we can't resist it. God makes us into a new creation. He changes us from someone who doesn't want God into someone who does. He changes our minds, so that we can understand the Bible and the truths it teaches. He makes us into someone different. Instead of a person who is unable to believe in Christ, we become a person who is unable not to believe.

For some reason, many people have a problem with this. They want to be responsible for their own salvation, at least a little bit. They want to feel that they were free to either accept God or reject Him. Really? Do they really want that burden? For if my salvation is mine to gain, it is also mine to lose; and I cannot be certain that I am strong enough to hold on to it. I am a very weak person and can be enticed by the sinful desires of this world. Perhaps some of those desires could pull me completely away from Christ. But thankfully, it's not up to me or you. God has called us to Himself, and it is up to Him to keep us in His hand, which He has promised to do. Even if we fail Him, He will never fail us.

Perhaps this is a new doctrine for you, and that's okay. This is honestly one of the most challenging doctrines of our faith. We pride ourselves on our independent spirit. We like to think we can take care of ourselves, that anyone can be anything he wants to be. We don't like the idea of losing control. So we have a problem in allowing even God to have total control over our lives; or to put it more accurately, we have a problem in acknowledging the control that God has over our lives.

But let's look at this from another angle. Have you ever prayed for someone else's salvation? If you ask God to save someone, what are you asking Him to do?

Now, if you believe that salvation is entirely the work of God, the answer is simple. You are asking God to perform that work in the life of that person.

But if you believe that salvation is up to the person, then what are you asking of God?

If you believe that the person must somehow recognize, on his own, the necessity for salvation and then come to God in faith, then why are you bothering God with it?

If you believe that a person can be called by God, but choose to reject His message, then what use is God? If man's will is stronger than God's, then what is the point of asking God to save anyone?

Does that make you feel a bit hopeless? If salvation is up to man, it is hopeless. But fortunately, it isn't up to man. It is up to God. All of it. God can do it, and we must trust Him in this. The fact that a person's salvation is entirely up to God is one of the most comforting doctrines in the whole of Scripture, especially to those of us who have lost a loved one. When we are certain that our loved one knew Christ, then we can rest assured that Christ will keep his promises and that our loved one is with Him.

But what if we are not sure that our loved one knew Christ? If you have had a loved one who passed on without knowing Christ, there is amazing comfort in knowing that it is God who is in control of these things and not us. We could not bear that responsibility. My husband and I have experienced several such losses, and it is this basic teaching that kept us going, even when the grief was almost too much to bear. Certainly, we should have talked to these dear ones more about Christ. Surely, we should have prayed for them more often. But no matter how much we failed in our duties, the responsibility for their salvation rests ultimately with God and not with us. We can always know that even at the very end of life it is possible for a person to be called by God, and we can hope to that end for those loved ones. God's timing is perfect, and I believe that sometimes He waits until the last moment to call a person to Himself. We have the example of the dying thief to attest to this. Finally, we must rest in the fact that God is God; He knows what He is doing; and He cares about us.

If you are still uncertain about this doctrine, then there are several passages of Scripture that I would point you to. First, look at Ephesians 1:3-6. Paul tells us here that we were chosen before the foundation of the world and predestined for adoption through Jesus Christ, according to God's purpose. Ephesians 2:4-9 adds that God made us alive with Christ while we were still dead in our sins [*my note*—not after we had received Christ], and saved us through faith, which itself is the gift of God.

Okay, that's Paul. What about the other New Testament writers? In I Peter 1:3, Peter tells us that Jesus Christ in His mercy has caused us to be born again. In his first letter, John tells us, "In this is love, not that we have loved God, but that He loved us and sent His Son to be the propitiation for our sins…We love because He first loved us."

And of course, I've saved the best for last. What did Jesus say about this? Quite a lot, actually, both directly and indirectly.

> Matthew 16:17—Blessed are you, Simon Bar-Jonah! For flesh and blood has not revealed this to you, but my Father who is in heaven.
>
> Mark 10:22— All things have been handed over to me by my Father, and no one knows who the Son is except the Father, or who the Father is except the Son and anyone to whom the Son chooses to reveal Him.
>
> John 6:44—No one can come to me unless the Father who sent me draws him.
>
> John 6:65—This is why I told you that no one can come to me unless it is granted him by the Father.
>
> John 10:24-26—So the Jews gathered around Him and said to Him, "How long will you keep us in suspense? If you are the Christ, tell us plainly." Jesus answered them, "I told you, and you do not believe. The works that I do in my Father's name bear witness about me, but you do not believe because you are not part of my flock."

Notice in this last passage, that Jesus could have said, "You are not part of my flock because you do not believe." But that is not what He said. They did not believe because they weren't part of the flock. They couldn't believe. Their minds and hearts had not been changed, and they could not understand the things of God. There are many other passages in the Old and New Testament that speak to this doctrine. The more you read the Bible, the more you will find.

So what about the passages like, "Whoever hears my word and believes Him who sent me has eternal life"? (John 5:24) Isn't this an invitation for anyone to come to Christ? Doesn't this mean that anyone can believe? Many years ago, I was in a Bible study with a young woman who was wrestling with that question, when she suddenly, in the middle of a study, realized the answer. Those verses are statements of fact. Of course, anyone who believes will have eternal life. And yes, in a sense, these invitations are for anyone. However, they are not statements of our ability to believe.

For example, I could tell you that anyone who can fly across the Pacific Ocean, on his own strength, without the aid of any other device, can have my entire bank account. And I could mean it. It would be a statement of fact. But that doesn't mean that you could do it. (And in case you're considering trying, my bank account is not worth the risk.) Anyone who believes will have eternal life. That is a promise of God, and He does not lie. However, the only way we can believe is for Him to change our hearts and make us able to do so.

Let me address another question that has come up from time to time. What if someone feels drawn to God but is afraid he or she is not chosen by God? My answer would be—it can't happen. Those who are not called by God don't want God. They want nothing to do with God. They are certainly not worried about whether He has called them. If a person feels drawn to God, it is probably because he or she is being drawn by God. I would pray with and for that person and encourage him to accept the faith to which God is calling him.

Does this mean that man has no responsibility, or that we are somehow excused if we do not accept Christ? Not at all. Scripture tells us that God has provided enough evidence of His own existence for anyone to believe in Him. No one is off the hook. As I have said in previous lessons, the reason people don't believe in God is simply because they don't want to. They want to have control over their own lives. They enjoy their sins, and they don't want to give them up. We are responsible for our own choices, regardless of the fact that we are unable to choose any differently. I know this doesn't make complete sense to us. But I also know that my mind does not work like God's mind.[21] We cannot understand God's thoughts in this, so we must accept what He tells us in His word. God has given everyone sufficient evidence to believe in Him; however, only those who are changed by the Holy Spirit will want to believe or be able to believe.

So if God has to change hearts, and it's all up to Him anyway, why do we need evangelists and preachers and missionaries? Because that's the way God wants it done. He wants us to share our faith. He wants some to do that in a particular, vocational way. Their life's calling will be to preach the Gospel or to minister to people in a special way. I urge you to support those who are undertaking that work. It is a unique calling, and worthy of our respect, but even more worthy of our gifts and our prayers.

But God calls all of us to tell others about Him, first through our lives, and then through our words. Our lives must come first, though. People must see Christ in our lives before they will believe Christ in our words. They must see the difference He has made in our lives and want that difference for themselves. We must meet people where they are, and accept them as they are, in order to gain a hearing for the Gospel. As Paul said, we may have to become all things to all people that we might win some to Christ.[22]

But even in our evangelism, isn't it wonderful to know that it's still all up to God? We can't argue people into the kingdom; we just need to let those around us know what Christ has done for us. And since that is pretty much everything, it shouldn't be too hard, should it?

12

LESSON 12
WHAT'S IN IT FOR ME?

Question 32: What benefits are there in this life for those who are effectually called?

Answer: ***Those who are effectually called partake in justification, adoption, sanctification, and the other benefits that, in this life, do either accompany them or flow from them.***

Question 33: What is justification?

Answer: ***Justification is an act of God's free grace, in which He pardons all our sins, and accepts us as righteous in His sight, only for the righteousness of Christ imputed to us, and received by faith alone.***

1. What did Christ do that made our justification possible?
   Read Romans 5:29; 3:24-25

Question 34: What is adoption?

Answer: Adoption is an act of God's free grace, by which we are received as sons of God, and have a right to all the privileges of that standing.

2. Why did God choose to adopt us as His children?
   Read Ephesians 1:5

3. Why should we not boast in our adoption as children of God?
   Read I Corinthians 1:26-30

Question 35: What is sanctification?

Answer: Sanctification is the work of God's free grace, by which we are renewed in the whole man after the image of God, and are enabled more and more to die to sin and live to righteousness.

4. Which person of the Trinity is primarily involved in working out our sanctification?
   Read 2 Thessalonians 2:13

5. How does God use our suffering to aid in our sanctification?
   Read Romans 5:1-5

Question 36: What are the benefits that in this life accompany or flow from justification, adoption, and sanctification?

Answer:* *The benefits that in this life do accompany or flow from justification, adoption, and sanctification are: assurance of God's love, peace of conscience, joy in the Holy Spirit, increase of grace, and perseverance to the end.

6. How do we know that we are assured of God's love?
   Read I John 4:9; Ephesians 2:4-5; I John 3:1

7. How do we know that we will not lose our salvation (that we will persevere to the end)?
   Read 2 Corinthians 5:1-5; John 10:29

Question 37: What benefits do believers receive from Christ at death?

Answer:* *The souls of believers are at their deaths made perfect in holiness, and do immediately pass into glory, and their bodies, being still united to Christ, do rest in their graves till the resurrection.

8. When do the souls of believers go to heaven?
   Read Luke 23:43; Philippians 1:23

Question 38: What benefits do believers receive from Christ at the resurrection?

Answer: At the resurrection, believers, being raised up in glory, shall be openly acknowledged and acquitted in the day of judgment, and made perfectly blessed in the full enjoying of God to all eternity.

9. What will happen to believers when Christ returns?
   Read I Thessalonians 4:16-17

10. What will happen to believers at the judgment?
    Read Matthew 10:32; 25:32-34

LESSON 12
WHAT'S IN IT FOR ME?

Catechism Questions 32, 33, 34, 35, 36, 37, and 38

MY FRIEND SANDY HAD A WRECK THE OTHER DAY. SHE WAS DRIVING out of a parking lot when a teenage boy, going about 60 miles per hour in a 35 mile per hour zone and talking on his cell phone, came over a hill and ran into the side of her car. Sandy had stopped and looked both ways before driving out of the lot, and her daughter Susan, who was a passenger in the car, had also looked. So who do you suppose was blamed for the accident? Sandy was, because she had pulled out into oncoming traffic.

That doesn't seem fair, does it? She was pretty upset about it too. She wanted to be vindicated. She wanted justification. She wanted to be declared not guilty. In her mind, and in mine as well, she was not guilty. But according to the laws of the state, she was at fault.

We can all imagine ourselves in Sandy's situation. We don't like to take the blame for something that is clearly not our fault. That is understandable. But we also don't like to take the blame for things that are our fault, like our sins. We want to rationalize those away. We want to be declared not guilty for those also. But we are guilty. The Bible tells us that we have all sinned, that none of us is good; none of us is righteous. We can't explain our sins away or minimize the seriousness of what we have done. We can't justify ourselves in the eyes of God.

We can't do it, but Christ can. He doesn't rationalize or minimize our sins, however; He paid the penalty for them. When He said on the cross, "It is finished," He was saying that it is all paid for. Every sin that you and I will ever commit has been paid for. We no longer owe that debt. We are free.

Now imagine that you have applied for a very important position. You send in your resume or CV and on it you have neatly printed your name and address. That's it. No experience, no education, no references. Just your name and address. You probably wouldn't even merit consideration for the job, but let's assume that for some inexplicable reason, the Human Resources manager decides to check you out. He searches the Internet, but finds nothing. He checks your social security number. There is nothing—there is nothing negative, but there is nothing positive either. You have no record of any kind. How likely is that you will get that position? Not very.

As Christians, without Christ's sinless life we would be in a similar state. We would have no record of sin, because Christ paid for our sins by his death on the cross. But we would have no positive record either. The Bible tells us that our righteousness is as filthy rags.[23] Our good deeds, done in our own strength and for our own purposes, count for nothing. So how can we earn a positive record? We can't, so Christ gives us one. His record of perfection is credited to us. That is justification. Not only do we carry no blame, we are seen in God's eyes as righteous, but only because of Christ. By receiving Christ as our Savior and Lord, we are justified.

We are also adopted. Perhaps you were adopted as a child, or maybe you have adopted a child of your own. I have friends who have both biological and adopted children and I honestly can't tell which are which. No one who just met the family would have any idea that one of the children was not a biological child. My friends who have adopted children have had such joy in their voices when they called to tell me that a child was waiting for them, that they were finally parents! When faced with an unplanned pregnancy, the gift of arranging an adoptive home is the most precious thing a woman can give her unborn child. I have known women who have made that choice and I honor them for it.

So some of us have been adopted by earthly parents, but if we are believers in Christ, then all of us have been adopted by God. There is an old hymn titled "I'm a Child of the King" and a contemporary Christian song called "My Father's House" which both express that idea. Our Father is God Almighty. He has adopted us. We belong to Him.

In the movie *Anna and the King* there are two scenes which I think illustrate this concept beautifully. In one scene, Anna is introduced to the King of Siam. She is told that her head must never be higher than his head. As the King sits down, everyone in the room bows lower and lower. The king is in total control; no one may enter his throne room or speak to him without his permission, on pain of death.

In a later scene, the king's oldest son gets into a scuffle with Anna's son. One of the king's daughters runs headlong into the throne room and into her father's presence, demanding that he come and do something about the fight.

He picks her up and carries her back to the scene of the trouble and solves the problem. She is not punished for entering the throne room without permission. She is not even reprimanded. Why? Because she is his daughter. He loves her, and she is allowed to come into his presence whenever she desires.

That is the way God treats us. He is the majestic King of the Universe, Ruler of all of Creation, King of kings and Lord of lords, yet we can run headlong into His throne room and beg for His help in whatever situation we may find ourselves. He will pick us up, carry us if necessary, and stay with us while the situation is being resolved. We are His children.

As His children, we are becoming more and more like Him. That is a long process called sanctification. We are gradually being made more like we should be and less like we have been. When we accept Christ, we are changed; we are new creations. But we are not sinless. God the Holy Spirit works in us to show us our sins and to help us to live a life that is pleasing to Him. There was a bumper sticker that I used to see that said, "Please be patient. God isn't finished with me yet." We need to remember that, not only for ourselves, but especially for others. God is not finished with them yet, either.

Because God has done these things for us—He has justified and adopted us and is sanctifying us daily—we can rest assured that He will continue to bless us. We are His children and He will never leave us. Nothing can separate us from His love. He will pour out His grace as He shows us what He wants us to learn and leads us in the ways we should go. We can have peace because we know that He is in control of everything that happens in this world, and He cares about what happens to us as individuals.

We can know that when this life is over, we will go immediately to be with Him. Our bodies may remain here, if we die before He returns, but our spirits will be instantly in His presence. My great-grandmother died of tuberculosis at a fairly young age, when my grandmother was only twelve years old. My grandmother told me that as her mother died, she sat up, raised her hands, and exclaimed, "Hallelujah!" I know that she is with Jesus now. Her body is buried in Texas, but her spirit is alive with Christ. I am looking forward to meeting her.

If we remain here until Christ returns, we know that He will come for us. The bodies of believers who have already died (like my great-grandmother) will rise first, then those who are still alive will be raised up, body and spirit. Our mortal bodies will be changed to immortal ones and we will be with the Lord forever. Paul tells us in I Corinthians that now we see things as though in a dim mirror. The writer of Hebrews tells us that this world is merely a shadow of the one to come, the one where we will live for eternity. Think of a dark house, with only a night light glowing. You can see things, but not distinctly. You can't really make out colors very well. Then when you turn on all the lights, how different things look. Colors are vivid and everything is clearly distinguishable. Right now, we are living in the dark. The night light is on, but we really can't see very well. In Heaven, all the light (the light of God Himself) will be on. We have no way of even imagining how wonderful that will be!

BOOKS ABOUT CREATION AND CREATION SCIENCE

Ashton, John F. *In Six Days: Why Fifty Scientists Choose to Believe in Creation.* Master Books, 2001.

Behe, Michael. *Darwin's Black Box: The Biochemical Challenge to Evolution.* Free Press, 2006.

Denton, Michael. *Evolution: A Theory in Crisis.* Adler and Adler, 1986.

Dembski, William, ed. *Uncommon Dissent: Intellectuals Who Find Darwinism Unconvincing.* Intercollegiate Studies Institute, 2004.

Ham, Ken. *The Lie: Evolution.* Master Books, 1987.

Johnson, Philip E. *Darwin on Trial.* Intervarsity Press, 1993.

Morris, Henry M. *Scientific Creationism.* Master Books, 1974.

Sarfati, Jonathan. *Refuting Evolution.* Creation Book Publishers, 2008.

Strobel, Lee. *The Case for a Creator: A Journalist Investigates Scientific Evidence that Points Toward God.* Zondervan, 2005.

Whitcomb, John. *The Genesis Flood.* P & R Publishing, 1960.

ADDITIONAL SCRIPTURES ON ELECTION/EFFECTUAL CALLING

John 6:38-39
John 10:28-29
John 17:1-3
Romans 1:6
Romans 8:30
I Corinthians 1:9
I Corinthians 1:23-24
Ephesians 1:11
I Thessalonians 1:4-5
I Peter 1:1-2
I Peter 5:10
I Peter 2:9
Hebrews 9:15
Jude 1:1

END NOTES

1 John 3:8
2 John 10:30
3 John 15:26
4 Exchanged Life, *http://www.exchangedlife.com/index.html*
5 Judges 4-5
6 I Peter 3:7
7 Luke 6:41-42
8 Romans 8:28.
9 Matthew 23:1-36
10 The Unification Church, *www.unification.org*
11 "Maharishi Mahesh Yogi, Spiritual Leader, Dies," *NY Times*, 02/06/08.
12 Revelation 3:16
13 Romans 1:24-25
14 Hebrews 2:17-18
15 John 7:5
16 Matthew 13:53-58
17 Hebrews 5:5-6
18 Hebrews 8:5, 9:24
19 John 10:17-18
20 Romans 14:10-12
21 Isaiah 55:8-9
22 I Corinthians 9:19-22
23 Isaiah 64:6

www.ingramcontent.com/pod-product-compliance
Lightning Source LLC
Chambersburg PA
CBHW030109070426
42448CB00036B/585

* 9 7 8 0 9 7 9 3 7 1 8 4 4 *